PROFESSOR
WAYLAND D. HAND
*of the University of
California at Los Angeles
comments on
The Legend of*
THE WANDERING JEW:

WITH fine scholarly insight Joseph Gaer has examined the corpus of legends that have sprung up about one of the world's most lonely and enigmatic characters, and has written an engaging account of his appearances and ministrations over the face of western Asia and Europe. . . . In this strange story of eternal wanderers and long sleepers, of watchers and waiters, there emerges a prefiguration of the tragedy of humankind, of the uncertainty of life, and even of death, and of the manifold problems of good and evil.

JOSEPH GAER was born in Russia and became a United States citizen in 1926. The author of more than twenty books and a member of the Screen Writers Guild, he has taught at the University of California and worked in the Government as well as private industry. His book How the Great Religions Began *is available in a Signet Key edition.*

Other Books of Special Interest

🪨 *The Legend of*
THE WANDERING
JEW 🪨

BY JOSEPH GAER

WITH EIGHT ILLUSTRATIONS BY GUSTAVE DORÉ

A MENTOR  BOOK
Published by The New American Library

COPYRIGHT © 1961 BY JOSEPH GAER

FIRST PRINTING, FEBRUARY, 1961

Library of Congress Catalog Card No. 61-9135

MENTOR BOOKS are published by
The New American Library of World Literature, Inc.
501 Madison Avenue, New York 22, New York

PRINTED IN THE UNITED STATES OF AMERICA

Contents

Plates

MEN'S minds are ruled as much by fable as by fact, as much by myth as by mathematics, and as much by legend as by logic. For the unknown is infinitely greater than the known, and in the realm of the mysterious, the imagination is a readier guide than the intellect. This was certainly true in the dim days preceding recorded history when man seemed to be preoccupied with many disturbing questions that he attempted to answer with theories, for which there was no proof, and in an infinite variety of legends, to which there is no end. The resulting treasury of myth and legend, tradition and saga, accumulated in early folk literature, or forklore, has become a great heritage; for this lore expresses all man's intrinsic fears and basic hopes, and in it is embedded man's unending search to discover hope in the midst of despair, purpose in the midst of chance, and order in the midst of chaos. The myths and legends that gave concrete expression to these fears and doubts and hopes have never wholly passed away from man's mind.

Some legends and traditions that arose out of the questions on the more profound and insoluble mysteries were more universally and lastingly accepted. Among these were the legends that attempted to explain the origin of life and the mystery of death, and man's relation to both. Wherever there were people capable of speech, there legends arose that gave proof of man's untiring preoccupation with those ever-present and never-explained wonders of being and not being—the one as mysterious and frightening as the other.

And among these more lasting legends there are few that have had such wide currency over so long a period as the Legend of the Wandering Jew. It has gone, as all traditions do, through repeated changes, assuming new symbolical meaning in each, while still retaining an essential core—the problem of redemption.

Next only to the question of the origin of life and of the enigma of death, man wanted to know very early how he should live in order to find favor in the eyes of his gods or god—and how he could atone for his selfish passions and weaknesses to gain personal salvation. The concept that man should seek his ultimate freedom, his ultimate redemption—in thought, in word, and in deed, acceptable to his conscience, to his fellow men, and to his god—this concept arose very early and was prevalent wherever man reflected on the meaning and purpose of life.

In folklore all abstract ideas are personified, and redemption was personified in the tradition of the Messiah. The Messiah is known in the folklore of different nations by different names, and is conceived of differently in the various legends that grew up. The legends went through many transformations, to serve new concepts of deathlessness and longevity, as either a blessing or a curse, and to accord with new theological interpretations of redemption.

The legends concerning the Wandering Jew most popular in the Western world are, naturally, Christian version, and they are in accord with the Christian concept of salvation. These legends revolve about a person who rejected or reviled Jesus in his hour of sorrow, and was doomed to wander over the earth until Judgment Day, or until he gained salvation through repentance. It is understandable that in the legends the man so doomed is presented as a Jew, since, in the days of Jesus, only Jews were either his Disciples and followers, or his repudiators and detractors. And this Jew so doomed must wander as a symbol to the world of the Second Coming—or as a symbol of the repentant sinner, or the unrepentant heretic.

A number of legends of the supposed appearance of the Wandering Jew are given in this book, in chronological sequence. It will be noted that there are signficant differences among them, which accord with the varying concepts of redemption. But most significant of all are the various names given to the Wandering Jew.

A name, in folklore, is never accidental and always symbolizes the character attributed to the individual. In ancient societies it was believed that the soul of a living being resided in the name. Children were given names which would bestow on them certain characteristics the parents wished them to have —in the hope that the name would act as a charm and an influence. Parents would call a girl "Ophelia" (meaning "snake") to assure that she would remain perpetually young and shed her years as the snake sheds its skin; or they would name a son "Bernard" (meaning "bear-strong") because they wanted their son to be brave and strong. Characters were given names in legends and the names invariably had significance, although it is not always clear now what the name was intended to convey.

In the legends of the Wandering Jew he was given a variety of names. He is called Malchus when he is believed to be the man whose ear Simon Peter cut off. In some legends he is called Cartaphilus, and is not a Jew, but a Roman porter in Pilate's court. In a very early ballad and in some recent novels, his name is Isaac Lakedion, or Lakadama or Laquedem, which might be a corruption of *L'kodem,* meaning the "ancient one." Joannes Buttadeus (John the God Smiter) is the obverse of Juan Espera en Dios (John Hope-in-God), and the Wandering Jew is known by both of these names. He is also known as Paulus, and Judas, and Athanasius, and Melmoth, and Theudas. In legends attributed to Mohammedan sources he is named Zerib Bar Elia (the Prophet Elijah) and also Michob Ader (the name on which, as we shall see, O. Henry built his tale). Other names too were given to him, both in the legends and in the literature based on them. But the name which appears most often is the most puzzling: Ahasuerus, or Ahasver. The underlying significance of this name, which appears in the Book of Esther, has puzzled all students of the legend.

The professions given the Wanderer also vary, as do his age and his traits of character—each influencing the intent of the legend. He appears most often as a ~~poor~~ or shoemaker or cordwainer. But he is also presented as a Roman soldier or a rich diamond merchant. In some legends he is old and suffers from the ailments of the very old—a state most deplorable; but others present him as one whose youth is renewed every forty or seventy years—a state most desirable. In many stories he, who denied and reviled Jesus, is Christlike in nature: he is humble, abstemious, gentle, helpful, noble in behavior and speech, a lover of children and beloved by them. Collectively, the legends present the Wanderer as a man in search of his soul—and redemption.

Stories of appearances of the Wandering Jew, the origins of the legend, and its reflection in literature and art are briefly examined in the following pages. It should be underscored, however, that in Part One of this book we are not dealing with historical and verifiable events, but rather with a redundancy of folk rumors about a legend that predates the Christian era by many centuries, full of inconsistencies in dates, the spelling of names, as well as the places where, presumably, events took place. S. Baring-Gould, in his pamphlet on the "Legend of the Wandering Jew," sums it up in these words: "The historical evidence on which the tale rests is, however, too slender for us to admit for it more than the barest claim to be more than a myth. The names and circumstances connected with the Wandering Jew and his doom vary in every account. . . ."

For those who may wish to explore the legend further, a brief annotated bibliography is appended. Some of the books given in the bibliography, in turn, will yield additional references, most of them obscure and out of print.

Part One

THE WANDERING
LEGEND

*"It is difficult to tell in any
of these cases how far the story
is an entire fiction and how far
an ingenious imposture."*

—Encyclopaedia Britannica

1. The Year 1000

THE year A.D. 1000 was anticipated by devout Christians with unprecedented awe and trepidation as well as with exultation. For in that year, the Christians had been told, the world would come to an end as had been foretold in the Scriptures.

Belief that the Second Coming of Jesus, to be preceded by Judgment Day, was imminent had strengthened the faith of the early Christians. Apocalyptic passages in the New Testament had been studied by these early Christians and interpreted to establish the time and circumstances of the Second Coming. Although leaders of that time were reluctant to set a specific date, they elaborated on the many signs which would appear to warn mankind of the approach of Doomsday—a day to which the devout could look forward with rejoicing, for it was to be followed by the establishment of the Kingdom of Glory on Earth.

During the period of Primitive Christianity, approximate dates for the Last Judgment were repeatedly set. And as each date passed without the appearance of the hoped-for events, an error in calculation was admitted, and the date was reset. The years turned into centuries, and the belief evolved that one thousand years—one day in the eyes of the Lord—would have to pass from the birth of Christ to the day of His Second Coming. And at the end of this period certain events would take place as unmistakable signs of the nearing Day of Judg-

ment—and the most reliable sign would be the appearance of the Antichrist. These beliefs were rooted in
Old Testament messianic concepts and were translated
into the language of Christianity by Christian eschatologists.

This belief that the year 1000 was to be the time of
the Second Coming thrived in the Near East, particularly among the common people of the Christian faith.
And as the last year of the tenth century A.D. drew near,
religious fervor revived among the believers, and many
Christians began to prepare for the Last Judgment by
giving away all their possessions and spending their
hours in repentance and prayer. They gathered in the
houses of worship and sang psalms; in particular, they
sang Psalm XC, underscoring and repeating,

> *For a thousand years in thy sight*
> *Are but as yesterday when it is past,*
> *And as a watch in the night*

—a passage that strengthened their faith by its millennial
implication. They recounted among themselves news of
the wars and rumors of wars among nations, the lack of
faith among the young, the sea of troubles all about
them, reminding each other that these things, as foretold by Jesus on the Mount of Olives, indicated the
imminence of the Day of Judgment. They scanned their
immediate environment for other signs of this imminence. And most of all they looked for the appearance
of the Antichrist—the one sign no one could ignore or
deny.

And the Antichrist did appear as foretold.

A stranger appeared, at first in Jerusalem, who openly "denied the Father and the Son." And he claimed
to be the Antichrist whom the Christians were awaiting.
Though he symbolized all that was evil, the people re-
joiced at this appearance of the Antichrist, for he was

welcomed as the harbinger of a great event: The Last Judgment was at hand.

The Antichrist was lonely and poor. And the Christians generously showered him with alms. Since they were disposing of their worldly goods as acts of charity and penance, they made the Antichrist their beneficiary. And the impostor, now masquerading publicly as the Antichrist, soon accumulated a great fortune. Like any shrewd rogue, he not only took advantage of the credulous but also clearly understood the importance of disappearing in time. As soon as his fortune was made, he vanished to enjoy his good fortune in parts unknown.

He had barely gone when another "Antichrist" made an appearance—and had the same good fortune.

Soon several "Antichrists" appeared in different parts of the city and in other cities and towns in the Holy Land. A number of rogues sensed how profitable it was to be an Antichrist in those times and in those parts, and the "Antichrist" began to appear everywhere. As soon as his fortune was made—and that was soon enough with people eager to rid themselves of possessions that soon would be useless—he disappeared as mysteriously as he had come, and his disappearance was accounted for by the explanation that the Antichrist was doomed to restlessness.

Stories began to circulate about these "Antichrists" which the imposters themselves may have suggested. The fact that so many claimed to be the Antichrist was ignored, and the belief arose that there was really only *one* doomed and cursed Antichrist, but that he appeared in different shapes. Each man, according to his own sin, saw the "Man of Sin" differently. He appeared tall to some, and small to others; one man saw him thin, and his neighbor saw him fat. He was seen as long-haired, and he was seen as bald. Some saw him as a young man, and others saw him old. All the different strangers the Christians had seen and heard of, and on whom they showered their alms, were indeed the one Antichrist.

The people were generous to these impostors; and they were just as liberal in the number of stories about encounters with the "Antichrist" which circulated in the marketplace, in homes, and wherever men gathered.

The fateful year 1000 came and slowly passed, and the world continued on. The disillusioned Christians went back to the Scriptures to learn wherein their eschatologists had erred in their calculations. The only tangible results left the people were memories of the "Antichrist," whom they had seen with their own eyes and whose words they had heard with their own ears, and the slowly evolving and transforming legends about him. They now began to associate the stranger with Malchus, the servant of the High Priest, whose right ear Simon Peter cut off with a sword when Judas and the band of soldiers had come to arrest Jesus.

Gradually the legend began to crystallize: the vanished impostors were the wicked Malchus who had dared to lay hands on Jesus, and who had therefore been doomed to wander restlessly until Judgment Day.

All this reconstruction of the birth of this legend is surmise, based upon dim and barely distinguishable remnants that have been woven into word-of-mouth folklore. For no written records of these happenings exist anywhere, other than in the echoes that are discerned in the writings of much later chroniclers.

By the time the First Crusade reached Jerusalem (in 1097), the legend of Malchus the Wanderer was already well established and had been incrusted with many ornamental details borrowed from the vast treasury of Judaic lore. In some legends the Wanderer was nameless, called simply "The Man Doomed by Jesus." Or he was called the "Immortal Jew," or the "Wandering Jew." And when the men of the First Crusade returned from the Holy Land laden with booty and relics, they brought back with them also a host of conflicting tales about a Deathless One who was doomed to wander over the earth until the Day of Judgment.

2. Visitor at St. Albans

THE first written account of the Legend of the Wandering Jew was chronicled at the great monastery of St. Albans, an abbey famous for its historians.

In the year A.D. 1228 a number of bishops and other church dignitaries gathered at the Abbey of St. Albans to authenticate additions to its collection of relics and to discuss, among other church problems, the then highly controversial topic of the widespread traffic in relics.

Among the foreign visitors at this gathering was an Archbishop of Greater Armenia, young-looking and soft-spoken. Though he spoke only through an interpreter, he captured the attention of all those present, and they listened to him with interest, for he had traveled far and had participated in many events. His mind was a storehouse of pertinent facts, which he knew how to sort and display as if they were jewels. And he had the gift of telling what his listeners already knew as if he were revealing new knowledge for which they had long hungered; and when he spoke of new and startling things, they sounded like revelations.

During a discussion on relics, he spoke glowingly of the relics of all kinds that he had seen in many places and vividly described them—from the tasseled girdle of Mary's that fell from the sky during the Assumption as witnessed by the Apostle Thomas, to the feather from the wing of the Angel Gabriel.

When the discussion turned on the magnificence of the Abbey of St. Albans in which they were gathered, and some wondered when it had been founded and what it had looked like at that time, the Archbishop of Greater

Armenia recalled the martyrdom of St. Alban in A.D. 303,
and the humble church that had been built upon the
spot. Almost five hundred years later, he related, King
Mercia found the relics of the martyr and founded a
Benedictine monastery in the saint's honor on that hill
facing the River Ver. Then the Archbishop told them of
the circumstances that led to the building of the new
abbey, the most magnificent and important Norman
structure in England, if not in the world. The structure was
dedicated in 1115, said the Archbishop, and he foretold
that what had happened at the Abbey of St. Albans in the
past would be surpassed by the great events still to take
place at the Abbey of St. Albans in the future.

The bishops and the other guests at the convocation
sought him out during their free moments and plied him
with questions on many topics; and he invariably rewarded them with memorable replies.

As the Armenian Archbishop was completing his description of Noah's Ark, preserved, he said, on one of
the Armenian mountains he had climbed, he was asked
whether in his travels he had ever come across or heard
anything of the man who, it was claimed, had witnessed
the Crucifixion of Christ and was doomed to wander
until the Last Judgment.

After a long pause the Archbishop said: "Strange
that you should ask this of me. For shortly before I left
Armenia this man, Joseph by name, dined with me."

The bishops and monks looked at each other in con-
sternation. And then they all tried to ask questions at the
same time, and no one could be heard. When the hubbub
subsided, this is the story the Archbishop told.

The name of the Wanderer at the time of the meeting
with the Archbishop was Joseph, and he had been wandering for nearly twelve centuries. In the days of Jesus
his name was Cartaphilus, and he had been a Roman
porter in the hall of Pontius Pilate. After Pontius Pilate
sentenced Jesus to be crucified, and as Jesus left the
Hall of Justice, Cartaphilus struck Him on the

back, shouting in mockery: "Go faster, Jesus, go faster! Why do you loiter?" Jesus looked at him and said: "I am going, but you shall wait until I return."

And since that day Cartaphilus has waited for His return. At the time of the Crucifixion, Cartaphilus was thirty years old. Ever since that time he grows older until he reaches the age of one hundred years; then he awakens one day to find himself again the same age he was at the time he struck Jesus.

"If his name was Cartaphilus," the Archbishop was asked, "why then did you say he was called Joseph when you saw him?"

The Archbishop explained that not long after the Crucifixion Cartaphilus suffered remorse and was baptized by Ananias—the same Ananias who had baptized the Apostle Paul. And at that time Cartaphilus was renamed "Joseph."

The Archbishop stated that he had seen Joseph on several occasions, at which time he had carefully interrogated him to determine whether there was truth in him, and had found him to be without fault. Joseph was a man of few words; he did not speak unless spoken to; and he spoke on religious topics only. He told of all he had witnessed after that day in Pilate's court; he described the suffering of Jesus during the Crucifixion; and told of the Resurrection itself. He also related in detail the dispersion of the Apostles to spread the Good Tidings.

"Joseph speaks always without smiling," the Archbishop recalled, "as one who is well practiced in sorrow and the fear of God."

"Have others spoken to him and questioned him?" one monk asked.

"Many come to him from different parts of the world," the Archbishop replied. "And to them, if they are men of authority, he resolves all doubts on any matter which troubles them."

Some of the Archbishop's audience still suspected that Joseph might be one of the impostors who claimed to be the Antichrist so that they might grow rich on the generosity of the credulous. To lay these doubts at rest, the Archbishop added: "He refuses all gifts offered to him, and is content with a little food and clothing. And he places his hope of salvation on the fact that he sinned through ignorance."

This account by the Archbishop of Greater Armenia is given in part, in the *Chronicle of St. Albans Abbey* kept by Roger de Wendover, one of the monks at St. Albans. When Roger de Wendover died in 1236, another Benedictine monk, Matthew Paris, completed and extended the *Chronicle*. The record as we have it today was completed about 1250.

Apparently, however, the story told by the Archbishop of Greater Armenia began to gain currency. For even before the *Chronicle* of Paris was completed, the Bishop of Tournai, Philippe de Mousket, composed in 1243 a rhymed version of the appearance of the Wandering Jew, based on the story told by the Armenian Archbishop.

The story of Cartaphilus' appearance, testified to by so venerable a person as the Archbishop of Greater Armenia, and recorded by such trustworthy and respected monks as Wendover and Paris, was accepted by many without question. With some variations in the telling and retelling, the story began to circulate and travel. It reached France and Germany and the Low Countries; and the farther the story traveled, the more it was believed, and the richer became the elaborations with which it was embellished.

Yet it was essentially the same story as told and recorded at St. Albans, except that in the Flemish version a variation of the name of the Wanderer appeared, and he was called Joannes Buttadeus (John the God Smiter). Nowhere has there appeared any convincing explanation of how "Cartaphilus" (beloved by God) turned into "Buttadeus" (smiter of God).

3. The Weaver's Apprentice

ALMOST three centuries passed before another appearance of the Wandering Jew was reported.

In the days when Ladislas II ruled over Bohemia, there lived in Prague a man named Kokot, who, like his father and grandfather before him, was the royal weaver. Kokot lived with his wife and children in a cottage not far from the palace. There, in a room which housed the royal loom, he worked from early in the morning until late at night, sending the boat-shaped shuttle carrying the weft through the shed, stopping from time to time to roll the clothbeam—and to sigh. As often as Kokot stopped to tighten the beam, he sighed. This went on all day long and every day he worked. For Kokot's heart was heavy and his mind plagued by a puzzle he could not solve, though it constantly rankled in his mind.

For when Kokot was a youth he had learned from his father that his grandfather had amassed a fortune in gold and silver, which he had carefully hidden on the premises of the very cottage in which Kokot was born, and that this treasure was intended for Kokot. The father explained that the treasure could not be given to Kokot before he reached manhood, and promised that Kokot would be told on his twenty-first birthday where it was hidden.

But before that day arrived Kokot's father was waylaid by men who had learned of the inheritance and demanded that he lead them to it. When he refused, they killed him, and the secret was buried with him.

After his father's death, Kokot devoted himself to

19

searching for his grandfather's treasure, working in secret throughout the night. But all his efforts were in vain. He could find no trace of his rightful inheritance.

In time Kokot married, and he was soon forced to devote himself to the task of earning a living for himself and his family, and could no longer afford to spend his time in speculation and in searching for the hidden inheritance.

Luckily Kokot had been taught a good and honorable trade. But his days were embittered by the belief that somewhere near him, in the cottage in which he labored, there lay a treasure that could free him from daily toil and bring honor and joy to all the days of his life.

Often late at night, tired from the day's work, Kokot would remain in his workroom long after his wife and children had gone to bed. He would brood about his inheritance, and once more repeat his search. But it invariably ended in frustration.

His wife and his friends doubted that the treasure had ever existed. They tried to explain the grandfather's will as a hoax on the part of the old man. Soon Kokot began to be afraid to even speak of the treasure to his friends, for they had begun to twirl their forefingers near their temples when they saw him. Yet Kokot's faith in the existence of the treasure was never shaken. As the years passsed he became interested less in the value of his inheritance than in finding out where it was hidden, to prove to his wife and to his friends that it was not an illusion.

Late one wintry night in the year 1505, so the story runs, Kokot was working at his loom, sending the bobbin shuttling back and forth, mechanically tightening the reed down after each row, and brooding, as was his wont, on the regret that his grandfather had ever left him a fortune which had served only to embitter his life and to make him the laughingstock of his friends.

Suddenly a soft hesitant tap upon the street door startled Kokot. He wondered who might be calling so late. And as he wavered, the knock was repeated, louder and more insistently. Kokot unbolted the door and slowly opened it.

In the doorway, against the black of the wintry night, stood a tall, gaunt, bearded man, wearing clothes too thin and worn for such harsh weather. The weaver's eye could see at a glance that those clothes, though ragged from age and wear, were of an ancient and excellent workmanship, such as he had never seen. The stranger's gray head was uncovered; his feet were bare; and he leaned forward a little, supporting himself with both hands on a staff.

The two men looked at each other for a long moment. Kokot gazed with surprise into the stranger's eyes—two deep pools of sorrow—and his heart sank. Finally Kokot bid the stranger come in and close the door behind him against the penetrating cold. The stranger entered the room, with the dignity of an expected guest, and looked slowly about, like one trying to recognize a place he had visited long ago.

Kokot observed the stranger carefully. Then, to cover his sudden embarrassment at gazing with his mouth half-open, Kokot plied the stranger with questions: Where did he come from? When had he arrived? What did he want at this hour of the night?

The stranger answered the questions, but without using a superfluous word. His name was Joseph. He came from afar. He had just arrived in Prague. He was tired and wanted lodging for the night. He had seen the light in the window and felt too tired to walk any farther.

Kokot noticed that the stranger's voice was soft and low. And though the stranger spoke in perfect Czech, his phrases sounded as if he were translating from an ancient language. At first the weaver offered to awaken his wife and have her prepare food for the old man; but Joseph would not hear of it. Then Kokot brought him some bread and cheese. And as the stranger ate, the weaver prepared a bed for him in the workroom.

The next day Joseph remained in Kokot's house and he won the affection of Kokot's family as soon as they saw him. Joseph helped Kokot at the loom, and showed great familiarity with the art of weaving.

"Why don't you remain here awhile?" Kokot suggested. "You can help me at the loom, and I will give you the pay of an apprentice, and you can live with us as one of the family."

Joseph accepted the offer and settled down to work. He labored long hours. And when he was not disturbed, he would pray as he worked. In the afternoons he would pause and gather Kokot's children about him to tell them stories about Jesus. The stories, with fascinating details, were related as if his own eyes had seen the events of which he spoke. When the children of the neighborhood learned of old Joseph's stories, they gathered in Kokot's yard to listen with rapt attention. And even the elders put down whatever they were doing, and they too listened.

Not long after Joseph had come to live with Kokot, the weaver, trusting him completely, confided to him the story of the fortune his grandfather had left and his unhappiness at never having found it.

Joseph interrupted Kokot before he had finished, and said: "Yes, I know."

Kokot stopped weaving and said, "What do you know?"

"I know where your grandfather's treasure is hidden," replied Joseph. "Your grandfather lived in this very house. And before he died he had a visitor. The house was different then, and yet the same." He looked around him to observe the changes. "Your good grandfather took in this old man and gave him a roof over his head and the food of his table to eat, just as you have done for me. And one day your grandfather confided his wish to hide all his wealth as a legacy for his grandson. The visitor helped your grandfather hide it; then the visitor left Bohemia. Later, the visitor learned that your grandfather had died and your father was murdered."

"But how do you know all this?" Kokot demanded.

"I was that visitor," Joseph replied.

"But that was so many years ago!" Kokot protested.

Joseph nodded. "I know." And after a moment's silence, he went on. "I am Joseph. But long ago my name was Cartaphilus, and I was a Roman porter in Pilate's court. I am the Wanderer who cannot rest and must roam over the earth in wretched poverty until Judgment Day."

"I do not believe it!" said Kokot.

"I can prove it to you," said Joseph.

"How?"

"I can show you the hiding place of your grandfather's fortune, which I helped him hide when I was last in Bohemia."

Then he led Kokot out into the yard. Together they cleared away an embankment near the cottage, three measured feet from the casement of the center window. There Joseph proceeded to dislodge bricks at the base of the wall. When he had made an opening, he plunged his hand in, as if into a vault and brought out a dust-incrusted basket. In it were all the gold coins Kokot's grandfather had hidden so long ago.

In exultation, Kokot ran to tell his wife. Then he ran to tell his friends. And after that he went to tell all his neighbors. Now it was Kokot's turn to laugh at those who had mocked him for so long and thought him mad to worry about a fortune that, they said, had never existed. He carried the basket close to his chest and exhibited all the gold and tarnished silver coins; and he asked each friend to estimate their worth.

Kokot ran joyously down the street telling and retelling his story and receiving envious congratulations on all sides. At last he returned home, tired but happy.

"Where is old man Joseph?" his children asked as soon as Kokot entered the house. "This is our story hour," they complained, "and he isn't here. We want him to tell us another story."

Kokot and his children sought the old man every-

where but could not find him. Then they went into the
workroom, and Kokot looked in the corner near the
loom where Joseph always kept his staff. It was gone.
Without a parting word he had left them. And only
Kokot knew who the old man really was; and only he
understood why the old man had to leave them as he
had.

4. The Wanderer and the Magician

ABOUT twenty years after the Wandering Jew left
Kokot, the happy weaver in Bohemia (according to
one nubilous tradition), he paid a mysterious visit in
Florence to Europe's far-famed physician and renowned
occult scientist, Dr. Cornelius Heinrich Agrippa (often
called Agrippa von Nettesheim).

It is understandable that the names of Cornelius
Agrippa and the Wandering Jew would inevitably be
linked in folk imagination, for both were assumed to be
endowed with supernatural and diabolical powers that
incited fear and wonder.

Dr. Cornelius Agrippa (1486-1535) was a German
physician who early in his life became interested in
astrology, necromancy, alchemy and other occult sciences, an interest which involved him in difficulties with
the Church. To top it all, he was also a feminist, and in
those days taking such a stand was tantamount to being
a disciple of the devil. He lived a stormy life, wandering
constantly and restlessly from Germany to Italy and
from Italy to France—equally famed and defamed in
all three countries. He wrote many books and papers in
defense of his chemical experiments, his researches into
the occult, and his philosophic observations about com-

munication with the dead—all of which his detractors termed sorcery. He died in Grenoble in ignoble poverty. According to his biographer, Henry Morley, who appraised Agrippa's life and work more than three centuries after his death, he was a noble character, and his writings on occult philosophy (*De Occulta Philosophia*) and the nobility of the feminine sex (*De Nobilitate et Praecelentia Femini Sixus*) are documents of significance if seen in proper perspective.

Dr. Cornelius Agrippa spent days and nights in his laboratory, experimenting with many strange ingredients, mixing and testing sulphurous and dangerous elements, in the attempt to compel them to reveal their unique powers. And rumor imputed to him numerous diabolical inventions that he kept hidden from the world.

One day, so the story runs, Cartaphilus, the Wandering Jew, paid an unexpected visit to the great alchemist—with a most startling request. This incident was fully and delightfully recounted more than a century ago by David Hoffman in his voluminous *Chronicles of Cartaphilus, the Wandering Jew* (about which we shall have more to say later on). Here is the version of the incident that is given in Hoffman's *Editor's Histoirette* in the *Chronicles*:

"Our next acquaintance with the unhappy Jew is one of a very wonderful character; and is altogether so extraordinary, that we should much rather have expected to have found it among the monks of the seventh century, than connected, as it is, with a name of no small celebrity in the *sixteenth* century! I allude to the very famous interview he is said to have had with the renowned Cornelius Agrippa—himself a very wise man, and no little of a wanderer,—which, even in those days, was in itself regarded as a somewhat suspicious circumstance, especially if the traveller was at all addicted to the occult sciences, or, unfortunately, has gained to himself, from overmuch learning, the name of magician! . . .

"Imagine, then, the famed Necromancer, Cornelius Agrippa, buried in an abyss of thought—surrounded by

divers crucibles and alembics, with skeletons of various
animals that garnished his walls. Upon his table lay
some ponderous and worm-eaten folios, in confusion—
many strange mixtures of metals, placed in acrid fluids—
numerous amalgams upon his right and left:—also, the
Elixirs, the *Salts,* and the *Sulphurs*—the *Ammonias,* and
divers other ingredients of his potential and secret art!
A shelf, nigh at hand, was burthened with many small
vessels, the curious contents of which the shining labels
told,—such as, *Mandibularum liquor,* or the oil of jaw-
bones—*Mandella,* or the seed of black hellebore—*Fassa,*
or the herb Trinity, and very many others!

"The shades of night were gathering over Florence;
and the lovely valley of the Arno had yet some feeble
glimmerings of twilight reposing upon its green bosom,
as if reluctant to part with so much beauty, or to cloud
its charms by night's darker mantle. Suddenly, Agrippa
heard a low rap at his door:—a tall figure entered, with
much courtesy in his demeanor—nobly formed—mysterious and awful in his carriage, and whose eye could
ill be divined, and both *youth* and *age* were so strangely
blended, as were never before seen in any mortal countenance! No furrow was upon his cheeck, nor wrinkle
on his brow: his large dark eyes flashed with the bril-
liancy of early manhood, and yet with all the intellec-
tuality of long-experienced age! But his stately figure
seemed to have the weight of some years, and his hair
streamed upon his shoulders in ample locks of fleecy
white, blended with some of nearly jet black! His voice,
though he uttered only a sentence, was tremulous, but
melodious—soul-searching—and enunciative of the so-
briety of wisdom! A silken abnet, inscribed with many
oriental characters, encompassed his waist in several
ample and graceful folds: in his hand he held a palmer's
staff—upon his feet were gorgeous sandals, faded and
worn: on his shoulders was a purple Ephod, of rare and
exquisite workmanship, likewise the worse for time and
wear. . . .

"The eye of the Stranger was quick in resting a moment upon a graceful, but most intensely black dog; whose small and piercing eye shot forth the intelligence, more of man than beast; and whose general expression seemed to amble upon the very borders of humanity! Time and circumstances, at that instant, permitted to the Stranger no closer scrutiny of the remarkable animal: but thought is speedier than action,—and he could not shut out a rush of ideas, inspired in him by that devoted and much-famed attendant upon the great philosopher; for the Jew had heard of what the crude people so stubbornly insisted—that this jet black dog was naught but the very demon wherewith Agrippa wrought his marvellous deeds in the magic art! Still the Jew spoke no further words than at his first entrance; but gazed upon *Monsieur* (for so Agrippa had named his dog), then reposing at his master's feet, amidst many ponderous volumes and opened manuscripts on the floor around him! As the Stranger entered, and uttered a few words of civility, there was an eye of the dog keenly intent upon him, and the other upon Agrippa, seemingly to inquire of his lord whether he should give a kindly welcome to the Jew! A morsel was instantly cast to the noble beast (his well known signal of hospitality), and quickly the philosopher and his dog were on their feet, to welcome the approaching guest.

"Agrippa gazed involuntarily, for a moment, in silence and wonder mixed with awe, upon the high intelligence of the Stranger, whose eyes shone with unnatural luster in the evening dawn,—but whose countenance was pleasing to behold, and powerfully awakening—there being deep-laid sorrow, wisdom, and resignation, that seemed to reveal a tale of long-accustomed misery, entirely softened by the supremacy of mind!

"'Pardon me, O Agrippa! this untimous intrusion, so unbidden, upon your privacy,' at length said the Jew: 'thy vast fame hath reached unto the world's limits; and I could not leave this fair city without communing with

thee, its brightest ornament—so loved by some, and so
dreaded by others!'

" 'Thrice welcome art thou, O Stranger,' said Agrippa,
'but thy curiosity in thus seeking me, will, I fear, be ill
requited; for fame is often mendacious, whether to *praise,*
or to *censure;* and to Agrippa it hath been both. My many
years have been more devoted to profitless and vain
pursuits, than in the gain of enduring honour, and of real
wealth: it is not all *regulus* that hath remained at the
bottom of my crucible, O Stranger!'

" 'Dost *thou* talk of many and tedious years, O learned
and renowned Agrippa!' exclaimed the unknown one,
'dost *thou* who hast scarcely seen more than three score
years, talk of lengthened life, spent in much thought and
vexation? I do remember me that, when quite a youth, O
Agrippa! I used to gaze upon the bright orb of day as
he declined,—and thought with delight of his speedy ren-
ovation in the far East, after he had quenched his rays
in the boundless waters! and then foolishly coveted that
my life should be like unto his—and be for ever! But,
my Agrippa, a young head can *wish* for more than old
shoulders can *endure,*—and long experience hath taught
me that far better is it to slumber among those tombs on
the Arno's banks, than, like the sun, to rise into reno-
vated life, and thus, for ages, to pursue the same dull
and toilsome existence:—But the tyrannous destiny of
that Sun is *mine!'*

"Agrippa shrank within himself, as the thought flitted
through his mind, that a dangerous madman was possibly
before him! But the Stranger mildly continued, 'I fear I
trouble thee with my visit, and by my unwonted speech,
that hath been too much of my poor self.' 'You indeed
hast puzzled me much, good Stranger,' rejoined Agrippa.
'Not so much, O Agrippa, as you makest *me* wonder, if
report doth not belie thee—and, if thou wilt grant my
request. I would have thee tell me of that MARVELLOUS
MIRROR, which thy potent art of magic hath enabled thee
to make—the renown of which hath brought even me,

Cartaphilus (for that is the name I bear), within thy door, seeking after such strange knowledge. Tell me, I pray thee, is it indeed true that whosoever looketh into that mirror, with faith, does see therein the *far-distant,* and the *long dead?* If so it be, then much doth Cartaphilus desire to look into that truthful mirror, since his eyes are wholly closed upon such far distant scenes. . . . To me, O Agrippa! all life is but as a vale of tears: myriads of myriads easily die—and *when,* and as they *would not:* but Cartaphilus follows not—rivers do change their course—the solid rocks do disintegrate— the mountain tops repose, at length, upon the bosom of the valley—the proud mausoleums resist the elements only for a time, and even the solidest of them do fade away at last! *Not so with me!* O give me therefore, I pray thee, but one look into thy much famed mirror, so that my earliest life—the one of my *real* youth, may again be seen of me.'

"Agrippa was greatly moved—but at length replied, 'Whom wouldst thou see? oh, wonderful man!' 'Son, or daughter, never had I at that time,' answered the Jew, 'but earnestly do I crave to see REBECCA, only daughter of Rabbi Eben Ezra—a princess of every virtue, and the most beloved of all Jewish or other maidens. I would behold her, as she was in youth—before Shiloh was fully revealed:—*as she was,* I say, when with her I wandered, as Cartaphilus, son of Mariamne, upon the flowery banks of the Kedron, in her father's garden—or, as we rambled in joyous carelessness, and with the boundless innocence of earliest mutual love, upon the heights of Ramoth-Gilead.'

"Agrippa trembled as the aspen: 'Who, and what art thou? and whether of Gehenna, or of Paradise, I wot not: but thy petition shall be essayed, come what may from the *nether* world,' exclaimed Agrippa with tremulous lips —whereupon he incontinently chaunted much strange language—and then he polished his mirror with the softest furs . . . and many lights of various colours were

seen streaming in from all directions! Agrippa then suddenly arose, raised his arms aloft towards Heaven, and
anon depressed them towards Gehenna; when lo! quick
as a meteor bursts, a mass of dazzling white light shone
around, and the mirror sparkled as the meridian sun!

" 'Thou art seemingly of but few years, compared with
what thou sayest,' cried Agrippa, 'and the mirror cannot
be faithful, unless my *wand* shall waive once, for every
ten years since the maiden lived:—proceed now, O
strange man! to number these *tens,* since last she
breathed . . . : and be thou most *faithful* not to deceive
me.' As bidden, the anxious and soul-wrapped Jew num-
bered 149 times! Agrippa gazed in maddening terror; and
at length sank with exhaustion upon his couch. 'Wave
on! wave on!' sternly yet imploringly exclaimed the Jew.
The wand soon continued to move, and but twice more—
noting thereby just 1510 years in all—when lo! the mirror's surface was filled with numerous forms, reflected
from its shining disk, seemingly as large as life, upon the
gossamer veils that encompassed the mirror! All those
forms were in the habiliments of ancient Palestine—each
engaged appropriately in rural sports and actions! Upon
the sweet scene the Jew gazed in wild rapture, as if his
eyes would devour what his arms could not embrace!
In the distance were lofty mountains, aspiring to kiss
the clouds; and hard-by was descried Ramoth-Gilead, an
ancient City of Refuge! In the foreground was a luxurious
valley, garnished with various goodly flowers, and re-
freshed by a limpid stream, gushing through wide crevices
of rocks, and anon, gently laving the banks—upon which
were seen indolently reposing many fleecy sheep, a
tamed gazelle, and numerous domestic animals—the cher-
ished pets of a female of matchless beauty,—who then
was sheltered from the noon-tide sun, by lofty cedars
grouped there by nature's tasteful hand. ' 'Tis she!—'tis
she!' cried the enraptured Cartaphilus, 'yea, Rebecca as
she was in the days of the then *Holy Temple*—a work
of human art the greatest and loveliest—as was *she* the

perfectest of nature's gifts! I must, I will *speak*.' Cartaphilus spoke to her! and lo! instantly thereon, the charm
was dissolved; a cloud gathered over the mirror; the dazzling light had wholly vanished; and the mysterious Jew
sank, as one senseless, upon the couch!

"Reviving, after a time, he seized the hands of Agrippa,
and said, 'Oh, many and boundless thanks to you, learned
Agrippa—thou Prince of all the Magicians! I pray you,
receive this purse of costly jewels. In it thou wilt find
more of value than in any other within my abnet—and
worthily do I bestow it on thee.' 'No!—No!' exclaimed
Cornelius Agrippa. 'Keep thy jewels, of whatever worth;
I will have none of them—no *Christian* man, perhaps,
dare receive them: but tell me, I do implore thee, *who
thou art? . . .*

" 'No peril to thee is either in my will, or in my power,
most worthy Cornelius Agrippa,' replied the Jew. 'My
name thou already hast; but *that* reveals me not unto
thee, as it seemeth. But now behold! I pray thee, that
exquisite *painting* suspended on thy walls, upon the left:
doth it not represent the SAVIOUR bearing his Cross?—
and look further upon thy right; yea, at that *portrait*
and then *upon me!*' Agrippa was lost in wonder; for the
likeness was indeed perfect! 'That portrait, O mysterious
man!' said Agrippa, 'is the faithful representation of that
wretched infidel who smote the Saviour and urged him
on when groaning under the weight of his Cross.' ' 'Tis
I—'tis CARTAPHILUS, the miserable Wanderer now before
thee!' exclaimed the Stranger, and instantly rushed from
the chamber. Agrippa retired to his couch, but not to
sleep."

Such is the story of the appearance of the Wandering
Jew in Florence, in 1525 or thereabouts, and his strange
visit with the far-famed magician, Dr. Cornelius Heinrich
Agrippa.

5. Fadilah and the Stranger

A SHORT time after the Wandering Jew visited the famed alchemist Cornelius Agrippa, he appeared in the East to the Moslem leader, Fadilah, during the sixteenth century.

After the Arabs under Fadilah had captured the city of Elvan, according to Sabine Baring-Gould (who, in turn, bases himself on the authority of Herbelot), Fadilah, who had led three hundred thousand cavalrymen into the successful battle, ordered his men to pitch camp in a protected area between two mountains in that neighborhood, and retired to his camp for prayer. It was evening, and when he was left alone he knelt, closed his eyes, and raised his voice in prayer:

"Praise be to Allah, Lord of the Worlds,
The Beneficent, the Merciful——"

In the distance Fadilah heard a faint voice, but he could not make out what it said or from where it came. And he went on with his prayer:

"Owner of the Day of Judgment,
You we worship and of You we ask for help——"

Again the voice now nearer and louder, interrupted. "*Allah akbar!* [God is great!]" Fadilah waited for a moment and listened. Then he continued with his prayer:

"Show us the straight path,
The path of those whom You have favored,

32

[I] *The Wandering Jew in Brussels*

[II]   *The Wandering Jew at the Flemish Inn*

[III] *The Wandering Jew Fording the Rhine*

[IV] *The Wandering Jew in a Swiss Valley*

PRINTED BY C. DICE.   ENGRAVED BY H. PISCHARD.

[V] *The Wandering Jew in Search of the Black Knight*

[VI] *The Wandering Jew in a Shipwreck*

[VII] *Wandering Through a Defile in
the Andes*

[VIII]   *Release at Last on Judgment Day*

And not of those who deserve Your anger——"

The voice now clear and near, called out again, *"Allah akbar!"*

Fadilah, convinced that this was not his imagination, cried out: "O thou! whether thou art an angel or whether thou art of another order, it is well. The power of God be with thee! But if thou art a man, then let mine eyes light upon thee, that I may rejoice in thy presence and society!"

Fadilah had scarcely finished speaking when a bald old man appeared in the tent. The stranger held a walking staff in his hands and resembled a very old dervish.

Fadilah rose and saluted the stranger, then asked him who he was and what he wanted. The old man, identifying himself as Zerib bar Elia (the Prophet Elijah), said: "I am here by the hand of the Lord Jesus, who has left me in this world that I may live therein until he comes a second time to earth. I wait for the Lord, who is the Fountain of all happiness.

When Fadilah heard these words, he asked when the Lord Jesus would appear a second time, and the old man replied that His appearance would mark the end of the world. Fadilah asked for the signs that would herald the approach of the world's end. And Zerib bar Elia gave him a detailed account of the social and moral conditions that would signal that the world's dissolution was near.

And here the record of the meeting between Fadilah and the Prophet Elijah ends, adding little to the Legend of the Wandering Jew. The episode does indicate, however, an early confusion between the doomed Cartaphilus and (as echoed in Mohammedan folk lore) the much more ancient Hebraic belief in the Immortal Prophet, Elijah.

6. The Bishop's Report

Toward the middle of the sixteenth century the Legend of the Wandering Jew became widely known through Germany. Oral reports began to circulate that trustworthy men had seen and questioned the subject of this legend. Several accounts reported him visiting different cities; and they varied only slightly in the description of the man, and his age, clothes, manners, former occupation, early family ties.

The major departure from previous reports was in the name: the Wanderer was now known as "Ahasuerus." (Though scholars have indulged in considerable speculation about this strange name for the Wandering Jew, they have come up with no convincing explanation.) And all the German accounts of that period about Ahasuerus seem to be variations on an oral report attributed to Paul von Eitzen.

When Paul von Eitzen, Doctor of Holy Scriptures and later Bishop of Schleswig, was still a student in Wittenberg, he returned on an Easter vacation to visit his parents in Hamburg. On that Easter Sunday to 1542 a cold wind blew and the people appeared in church bundled against the wintry day. Young von Eitzen shivered as he made his way down the church aisle, unwrapping his scarf and unbuttoning his coat. Suddenly he was struck by the sight of a strange old man near the railing of the chancel. He was inordinately tall and gaunt, with snowy white hair falling over his shoulders, and a beard reaching to his chest. Though the weather outside was bitterly cold, the stranger's feet were bare, his trousers were thin

and frayed at the ends, and he wore a threadbare and
outlandish cloak which obviously offered little warmth,
though it was tied tightly around his body. His lean and
narrow head was bowed, his eyes closed.

Paul von Eitzen could not withdraw his gaze from the
stranger throughout the service. The old man listened to
the sermon with concentrated attention. And every
time the name of Jesus was uttered, he smote his breast
with his fisted right hand. He gave no sign that he was
aware of the other parishioners around him, sitting there
as if he were utterly alone in the world.

At the end of the service, Paul von Eitzen and several
other theology students approached the stranger, full of
awed curiosity. The old man spoke to them freely, but
in a voice pitched so low that they had to strain to hear
him and in tones so melodious and cadenced that his
conversation sounded like a reading from an ancient
hymnal. He answered their questions without reservation
and with complete humility, in fluent middle-high-German.
And when some of the students questioned him in Latin,
in Hebrew, and in several European languages, he answered each question in the language in which it was
asked, showing equal familiarity with the idiom of each,
though in some of the languages his speech revealed a
decided accent.

Paul von Eitzen arranged to meet with the stranger
later, at a place where they could converse freely. And
when they met, the stranger disclosed that he was a
Jew, whose name was Ahasuerus, who was born in
Jerusalem in the year of the birth of Jesus. When he grew
up he became a shoemaker—as poor as any shoemaker
of his day.

Ahasuerus related his sad history in great detail:
Regarding Jesus as a heretic and one of the false Mes-
siahs common in those days he had joined the crowd
around Pilate's court during the trial of Jesus, and was
among the first to clamor for the release of Barabbas
and the condemnation of Jesus. He did this not out of

religious scruples, but out of personal resentment at the
claim made for Jesus by His Disciples that He was the
Son of God and therefore deathless. And, like Judas,
Ahasuerus wished to see the claim tested.

After the sentence was pronounced by Pilate, Ahasuerus hurried home to tell his family that Jesus had been
condemned and would soon be led down their street to
Golgotha for His Crucifixion. And, later, when his family
heard the crowd approaching, Ahasuerus took his little
son and placed him on his shoulders so that the child
might better see the procession of the condemned prisoner led by the Roman soldiers.

Jesus, stumbling under the heavy burden of the crossbar
of His Cross paused near Ahasuerus's house for a
moment's rest and leaned against the wall. Ahasuerus,
eager for the crowd's approving attention, called out:

"Go on, Jesus, go on! Why do you linger?"

And Jesus looked at Ahasuerus and replied: "I will
stand here and rest, but you shall go on and know no
rest until I come again."

Instantly, Ahasuerus put the child down, sending him
back to his mother, and followed Jesus for the rest of the
sorrowful journey. He remained at the foot of the Hill of
the Skulls until the Crucifixion was over. Then, when
the crowd began to disperse and return to the city,
Ahasuerus could not return to Jerusalem. He wandered
on and never saw his wife and child again. He felt
compelled to wander from one place to another and
from one country to another, stopping nowhere long
enough to make friends or to feel at home. He wandered
on in poverty and privation and in utter loneliness, year
after year and decade after decade.

After many years his wanderings brought him again
to his birthplace, but the Jerusalem he had known was
no more. It had been sacked and destroyed, and no one
in that desolate city had ever heard of Ahasuerus's
family or his kin.

The cursed Ahasuerus wandered on. In some places he

remained for a considerable time, in others for only a
few days. If anyone looked at him and smiled in friendly
recognition, and his heart yearned to remain in that
place—at that moment he was compelled to leave.

When he was questioned about the martyrdoms of the
Apostles, the decline of the Roman Empire, the Crusades,
the rise of the Hapsburgs, the medieval Inquisition, and a
host of other topics, Ahasuerus would recall clearly
where he was at the time of the event and describe it
from his own point of view. His accounts invariably
checked with the facts of recorded history, though his
interpretations of origin and effect often differed.

Ahasuerus remained in Hamburg for a while, and
Paul von Eitzen saw him often and spent many hours
conversing with him. Von Eitzen also brought with him
many learned men to question Ahasuerus and to test him
in matters of ancient history. And they all came away
astonished, but convinced that Ahasuerus was telling
the truth.

Paul von Eitzen found that the stranger ate and drank
just enough to keep body and soul together. And when
he was offered money, he refused to accept it. Whenever
people insisted on forcing gifts on Ahasuerus, he gave
whatever he received to the poor, claiming that God,
who knew his remorse, would provide for his needs. No
one ever heard him laugh. No one ever saw him smile.

Once the wanderer was asked why God wished him
to wander until Judgment Day, and he replied that perhaps God wanted him to serve as an example to the un-
believing and the unrepentant.

Paul von Eitzen told of Ahasuerus as an abstemious
and saintly person, a repentant sinner who sought by
example to bring mankind close to Jesus. He was referred to not as the Wandering Jew, but as the Eternal
Jew; and he was treated by everyone with respect and
even reverence.

Of course Paul von Eitzen did not record the encounter with Ahasuerus, *der ewige Jude,* at the time they met—nor even later when he became Bishop of Schleswig. The story of their encounter was kept alive and transmitted orally. More than a half century after the meeting presumably took place the account of it was finally written down, and made public in 1613, by one Chrysostomus Dudulaeus of Westphalia (the name is believed to be a pseudonym). By the time the writer using the pseudonym of Chrysostomus Dudulaeus of Westphalia put the chronicle down on paper, he could record several subsequent appearances of Ahasuerus in other places and under different circumstances, such as the following two episodes.

In 1575 Christoph Krause (or Christopher Elsinger) and Jacobus von Holstein were sent by the Duke of Holstein as ambassadors on a mission to the royal court of Spain. At their return they asserted with their solemn oaths, that they had come across the same Ahasuerus in Madrid. In appearance, manner of life, habits, clothing, and knowledge of the past, he was exactly as he had been described by Paul von Eitzen of Hamburg. They spoke with him in Spanish, and were satisfied that he was *der ewige Jude.*

About twenty-four years later (1599) a trustworthy and respectable citizen of Brunswick wrote to a respectable and trustworthy citizen in Strasbourg about the wonderful wanderer Ahasuerus who had been seen in Vienna and was preparing to go to Poland and Russia.

And, as if to give proof of the authenticity of this report, Chrysostomus Dudulaeus adds, "This Ahasuerus was at Lubeck in 1601, also about the same date in Revel in Litvonia, and in Cracow in Poland. In Moscow he was seen of many and spoken to by many."

At this stage in the growth of the Legend of the Wandering Jew Ahasuerus is represented as continually doing penance, claiming that he has touched neither food nor drink nor has closed his eyes in sleep for almost sixteen centuries—since the day of the Crucifixion.

7. The Ballad of Brabant

G RADUALLY the legend began to circulate in every part of Germany and Eastern Europe, and had become deeply lodged in folk imagination.

In some regions the Wandering Jew come to be regarded as a tragic figure, one viewed with compassion; and in each retelling of the legend a new trait was added to his character that made him more sympathetic and more appealing as a person. In many versions an attempt appeared to mitigate and lighten the Wanderer's burden.

The rumors that the Wanderer had been seen in Vienna, in Cracow, in Moscow and in Strasbourg traveled widely. He appeared in the most inclement weather barefoot and dressed in threadbare rags of a Roman make. He clung to his poverty and wretchedness, and when any gift was made to him, he gave it to those who needed it more. He was abstemious—or, in some stories, he had touched no food or drink in sixteen centuries.

To the folk imagination it did not seem credible that God would be so unrelenting to so devout and repentant a sinner, and the legend was amended to include circumstances when the Wanderer might find relief—to drink some water to slake his centuries-old thrist or to close his eyes in a new forgetful moments of slumber. It was said, for instance, that between early May and late July, when the moon was full and had a triple ring around it, the Wanderer, if he came upon two oaks that had grown together in the form of a cross, could lie under the oaks and fall asleep until the cock crowed. There

were special circumstances when the sorrowful Wanderer
might drink water—though the circumstances and for-
mulas differed from place to place and from retelling
to retelling.

In some countries, particularly as the legend traveled
westward, the Wandering Jew took on the qualities of a
sinister and embittered figure. He appeared only in
stormy weather, because storms and hurricanes surrounded him; and pestilence followed in his footsteps.
He was an unrepentant criminal deserving his punishment.
In such places he was spoken of in whispers. When a
storm arose, people gathered together to pray that their
town might be spared from a visit by the Wanderer.

And they, in turn, found certain fixed occasions when
the Wanderer might be kept from quenching his thirst,
breaking his fast, or finding relief in sleep. The people
were cautioned not to do anything that might be of help
to this Buttadeus—the God Smiter.

For instance, it was accepted, in some countries, as a
well-known fact that when the Wandering Jew came to a
field in which a chain harrow was left with teeth down-
ward, he could curl up near it and fall asleep. The thing
to do, of course, was to leave the harrows in the field
with their teeth upward, so that when the Wanderer came
by, he would be forced to go on.

Whether viewed as Joannes Buttadeus (John the God-
Smiter) or Juan Espera en Dios [John Hope-in-God],
he became immortalized in many legends; and his reported visits were often commemorated in long and
mournful ballads.

In 1575, the year that Christopher Elsinger and Jacobus
von Holstein conversed with Ahasuerus in Madrid, the
Wanderer also appeared in Brussels in Brabant, where
he related his sorrowful story in impeccable German,
and gave some details about his origins and his long life,
unrevealed in earlier interviews.

His visit to Brabant was commemorated in a very

long ballad that gained great popularity in its time and was translated into a number of languages.

In this ballad the Wandering Jew is treated with great sympathy; and for the first time we encounter the use of the name "Isaac Lakedion." (*Lakedion,* apparently a corruption of the Hebrew word *Lkodem,* meaning the "ancient one," was later transliterated into *Laquedem,* the name used in many fictional treatments of the legend.) In this ballad we learn that Isaac Lakedion was twelve years old when Jesus was born; how he was doomed; and how he had sustained himself throughout the centuries after giving up the trade he had followed in Jerusalem.

As often happens in folklore, one version of an event differs greatly from other versions of the same event, when translated and told in different countries, and on different occasions. The time an event took place and, in fact, what took place as given in one version may have little resemblance to another. The Wandering Jew's visit to Brabant is no exception. Different editions differ so greatly that it is sometimes difficult to realize they refer to the same ballad. David Hoffman and others date the Ballad of Brabant as 1575, and assert it recorded events that took place in that year. But the Addey (1857) edition of Gustave Doré's *The Legend of the Wandering Jew* gives the Brabant visit as having occurred exactly at six o'clock on the afternoon of April 22, 1772. What could be more specific?

All the accounts, however, seem to agree that the Wandering Jew's visit to Brabant resulted in a ballad of twenty-four stanzas, and that ballad is invariably called: *The Complaint of the Wandering Jew*.

Here are a few stanzas from this ballad:

> We used to think your story
> Was but an idle dream;
> But, when thus wan and hoary
> And broken down you seem,

The sight cannot deceive—
And we the tale believe.

Are You that man of sorrow
Of whom the authors write—
Grief comes with every morrow,
And wretchedness at night?
Oh! let us know, are you
Isaac, the Wandering Jew?

Then *he* replied—"Believe me
I suffer bitter woe;
Incessant travels grieve me,—
No rest's for me below;
A respite I have never,
But onward *march* for ever!

'Twas by my *rash* behaviour,
I wrought this fearful scathe;
As Christ our Lord and Saviour
Was passing to the grave—
His mild request I spurn'd,
His gentle pleading scorn'd.

A secret force expell'd me
That instant from my home;
And since, *the doom* hath held me
Unceasingly to roam,—
But neither day nor night
Must check my onward flight!

I have no home to hide me;
No wealth can I display;
Yet, Unknown Powers provide me
Five farthings every day!
This always is my store—
'Tis never less, nor more!

Here, in addition to the new name given the Wandering
Jew, we find the Wanderer is provided with a self-per-
petuating coin in his purse—a coin of such little value that
it would seem it could hardly provide for the Wanderer's

needs. Yet no sooner is it spent than another coin appears in his purse—to keep him from starving.

In later legends this coin becomes a subject of much speculation. In one legend it is the source of the Wanderer's great wealth; he adds one coin to another until he has enough to buy a diamond, and then one diamond to another, thus accumulating a great fortune that he carries in his belt.

8. Creutzer's Pamphlet

IN 1602, eleven years before Chrysostomus Dudulaeus of Westphalia published his chronicle of Bishop von Eitzer's experiences with Ahasuerus, the Wandering Jew, there appeared in Leyden, a pamphlet that gave the legend instant and meteoric popularity. The pamphlet, written by one Christoff Creutzer, was called *Kurtze Beschreibung und Erzehlung von einem Juden mit Namen Ahasverus* (*A Short Description and Story of a Jew named Ahasuerus*). Under such a mouth-filling title one would expect a tract of considerable proportions. But, in fact, Creutzer's "short description" was truly brief—barely four pages; actually it was a mere leaflet, that bore no publisher's imprint or even a printer's identification. Nor was Creutzer's story of the Wandering Jew new and startling, for it seems to have been based on Matthew Paris's chronicle of the story told by the Archbishop of Greater Armenia at St. Albans in 1228, and to have included the Paul von Eitzen report of Ahasuerus' visit to Hamburg in 1542.

Creutzer's pamphlet was an instant and startling success.

In *Die Sage vom ewigen Juden*, published in Leipzig in 1884, Herr Neubaur tells us that, within a comparatively short time, Creutzer's pamphlet went through forty-six editions in German, nineteen in Swedish, ten in French, four in Danish, three in Flemish, and that it was translated also into Polish, English, Czech, and other languages.

The publication and widespread popularity of Creutzer's pamphlet stimulated reports of the appearance of the Wandering Jew. In the cities and towns of Europe any old stranger was suspected of being the very Ahasuerus that Creutzer had described. In the marketplaces people began to scrutinize roaming beggars, searching for one who fitted the description of the man who had already lived sixteen centuries and was doomed to live on for an untold number of centuries to come.

The lowly contented themselves with verbal speculation about the Wanderer and what he signified. But people of education and breeding confided their encounters with the Wandering Jew, and their observations concerning him, to their diaries and journals. Some stated boldly what they had seen and what they had heard. Others wrote apologetically, fearing to repeat what they suspected might be labeled as gossip and superstition even in their day.

Such a one for instance, was Rodolphe Bouthrays, the parliamentary advocate of Paris, who recorded in his chronicles and commentaries in 1604: "I fear that some may charge me with anile trifling and giving ear to old wives' tales, if I insert here the story told in the entire of Europe concerning the Jew, who lived in the days of the Saviour Christ. However, nothing is more common and our popular histories have not scrupled to assert it. Following the lead of those who write our annals, I may say that he who appeared, not in one century only—in Spain, Italy, and Germany—was also seen this year (in Paris) and recognized as the same individual who had appeared in Hamburg in 1564. The common people, bold in spreading reports, relate many things of him; and this I allude to, lest anything be left unsaid."

In 1604, the same year in which Bouthrays recorded in his chronicles the rumored appearance of the Wandering Jew in Paris, a lawyer named Louvet, of Beauvais in the north of France, recorded this strange experience:

One Sunday morning, Lawyer Louvet was on his way to the then unfinished (and to this day unfinished) Cathedral of St. Pierre, the loftiest building in Christendom. The day was cloudy, and a strong breeze was blowing when Louvet left his house. But by the time he neared the cathedral the cold wind had reached such proportions that he had to plow his way to the cathedral with bowed head and straining body. The nearer Louvet came to the cathedral, the stronger grew the wind. And as he finally ascended the cathedral stairway the wind had reached almost the proportions of a hurricane. At the head of the stairs he almost collided with a stranger who stood near the wall for protection from the wind.

Louvet looked up in surprise at the gaunt old man with a flowing white beard and long white hair, dressed in rags. Though his clothes were those of a beggar, his dignified bearing instantly commanded respect. The old man was surrounded by a group of children, who having come early to church had gathered around to listen to the stranger; and he was speaking to them in a voice so low, and in such melancholy tones, that the children's eyes were filled with tears.

Lawyer Louvet glanced with horror first at the children and then at the stranger, then hastily entered the cathedral, aware that this was the stranger who had come to visit their city, according to rumor, on the wings of a storm.

Inside the cathedral Louvet found men in huddles whispering about the rumors of the stranger in their city. It was said that he had been a devout Christian ever since the days of the Apostles. It was said that he spoke against the Papacy. It was said the Church warned that, at best, he invariably brought with him bad weather and, at worst, the dreaded plague.

As Louvet listened to all the talk he determined to speak to the stranger, and resolved that as soon as the services were over he would go out and interrogate the Wandering Jew.

But when Louvet left the cathedral, the sun was shining and a light breeze was blowing. People were strolling about smiling, with their faces turned to the sun. Louvet looked about for the Wanderer but he was not to be found. Louvet asked people whether they had seen the Wanderer, and they replied that they had seen him earlier in the day but that he had since disappeared. All through the city, Louvet searched, but the Wanderer had gone. And he never returned to Beauvais.

A few years later Julius Bulenger, a citizen of the Netherlands, completed a history of his times which was published in Leyden in 1619. In it Bulenger reported the appearance of a Jewish contemporary of Christ who has been wandering about the world since the crucifixion of Christ. He had been condemned by God to roam without food or drink and to know no home anywhere, because he had been the first to cry out before Pilate for the Crucifixion of Jesus and the release of Barabbas. And he is also doomed because "when Christ, panting under the burden of the Cross, sought to rest before his workshop, for he was a mechanic, the fellow ordered him off with acerbity. Thereupon Christ replied: 'Because you grudge me a little rest, I shall enter my rest, but you shall wander without rest.' And since then, frantic and agitated, he fled through the whole earth, and on the same account to this day he journeys through the world." It is the same man—and Bulenger never names him— who was seen in Hamburg in 1564. And the historian adds with remarkable candor: "I did not see the man at that time, since I was occupied in Paris, nor did I hear about him from sufficiently trustworthy authorities."

Some twenty years after the publication of Bulenger's history, a pamphlet appeared that received considerable attention entitled, *Histoire admirable de Juif errant,* written by two citizens of Brussels, identified as residents of Gerberstrasse.

One day, the pamphlet records, two men of Brussels, walking through the forest of Soignes, met an aged man whose clothes hung in tatters and were made of a very ancient cloth. There was something about him, particularly the sadness of his face, that distinguished him from any mendicant they had ever met. In fact, he was not a beggar, for he asked nothing from them. They invited him to join them in a "refreshment house," and he did, but would not sit down with them. He remained standing as their food and drinks were served. He would not eat with them, but gladly answered their questions. His name, he said, was Isaac Laquedem—he was the same who had refused to let Jesus rest for a moment at his door, and for this he had been doomed to wander. At first the two burghers were incredulous. But as they plied him with questions and he related events that had happened many hundreds of years before, they became convinced that they were conversing with the Wandering Jew. They grew greatly agitated, and resolved then and there to record this encounter as soon as they returned to their home. Which they obviously did.

Although the Wandering Jew was frequently seen in different parts of Europe, travelers returning from the Holy Land told of seeing the Wandering Jew in Jerusalem. And the Jerusalemite Wandering Jew assured them that he had never left that city, for he had been doomed, not to wander but, on the contrary, to remain on the exact spot on which he had committed his great sin, to wait there until Jesus came again.

In Jerusalem, the returned travelers reported, the doomed sinner was imprisoned by the Turks. They had placed him in a very narrow cave, and he walked from wall to wall, beating his breast in penance. He could neither sit nor lie down to rest. He took neither food nor drink. He still wore the Roman clothes he had worn on that fateful day. He spoke only the language that he had known at that time, which was Aramaic. He spoke only in answer to questions. And all the time he paced back and forth, like a pendulum perpetually in motion.

Other travelers declared that although they had not seen the doomed man in Jerusalem, he was there. For the man was Malchus, and he had been doomed to circle *underground* around the pillar to which Jesus was bound when he was scourged. According to this legend, Malchus was among the Roman soldiers who took part in the scourging—but he, unlike the others, took pleasure in the task. And because of that he must circle the pillar until the Day of Judgment.

These reports by the Holy Land travelers prompted people to believe that there was more than one Wandering Jew. And in a pamphlet under the awesome title, *De duobus testibus vivis Passiones Christi,* by Martin Dröscher, published in 1668, it is argued that Cartaphilus and Ahasuerus are really two distinct persons, one of whom is doomed to remain in the Holy Land, the other to wander all over the world.

Another pamphlet states that there are indeed two Wanderers, but they are a man and his wife. For both Cartaphilus and his wife, according to this claim, took part in urging Jesus to move on. And after that moment both husband and wife became vagabonds, wandering in opposite directions and meeting for one brief hour once every hundred years. Throughout a century they dream of the day on which they will meet, when they will see a face each will recognize. But they no sooner meet than their hour of joy is embittered by the thought of their imminent parting for another hundred years.

In forested areas the Wanderer was often seen as a

wild and dangerous huntsman who haunted deep recesses. And when a storm arose in such areas, the people would look out of their windows and say that it was the Wild Huntsman, the Wandering Jew, passing nearby.

There is a Swiss story that one day the Wanderer stood below the Matterhorn, looking about him with sorrow and wonder. A mountaineer standing nearby asked the Wanderer why he seemed so astonished and sad. To this he replied that he had been on that very spot centuries before, at which time a flourishing city had covered the site. Now it was covered with gentian and wild flowers, with not a sign left of the city that had been there. Then he added that he expected to return to that site again, and that would be on the eve of the Last Judgment.

Each report of the Wandering Jew's appearance stimulated new interest in him. Each pamphlet or written record about him encouraged new speculation and resulted in new theories. And the legends multiplied with infinite variations.

9. Report of the Turkish Spy

IN Paris in the year 1644 there lived a spy for the Turkish government, who, undoubtedly, was known by many names, as is the custom among spies. He reported to his superiors on such secrets of the French government as he could obtain, on whatever he could learn from other spies in Paris working for other governments, on brother spies whom he suspected of disloyalty and of trying to sell Turkish secrets to the French, and on various other matters of interest to the Turks.

One of the Turkish spy's reports, sent to a lawyer named Ibraham Haly Cheik, is of particular interest to us, for it is devoted to one Michob Ader, who had been an Usher in Pilate's Court of Judgment. The Turkish spy reported that he had personally interviewed this Michob Ader, particularly on what he knew of Moslem countries; and he ended the report with the suggestion that the man was an impostor. Moncure Conway, in his book *The Wandering Jew,* gives this report in its entirety; and in its entirety it is reproduced here:

"Paris, 4th of the 1st Moon of the Year 1644.

"There is a man come to this city, if he may be called a man, who pretends to have lived above these sixteen hundred years. They call him the Wandering Jew. But some say he is an imposter. He says himself that he was Usher of the Divan in Jerusalem (the Jews call it the Court of Judgment), where all criminal causes were tried, at the time when Jesus, the Son of Mary, the Christians' Messias, was condemned by *Pontius Pilate,* the Roman President. That his name was Michob Ader; and that for thrusting Jesus out of the Hall with these words, 'Go, why tarriest thou?' the Messias answered him again, 'I go, but tarry thou till I come'; thereby condemning him to live till the Day of Judgment. He pretends to remember the Apostles that lived in those days, and that he himself was baptized by one of them; that he has travelled through all the regions of the world, and so must continue to be a vagabond till the Messias shall return again. They say that he heals all diseases by touching the part affected. Divers other miracles are ascribed to him by the ignorant and superstitious; but the learned, the noble, the great, censure him as a pretender or a madman. Yet there are those who affirm that 'tis one convincing argument of the reality of his pretence that he has hitherto escaped a prison, especially in those countries where the authors of all innovations are severely punished. He has escaped the Inquisitions at Rome, in Spain, and in Portugal, which the vulgar will have to be an evident miracle.

"One day I had the curiosity to discourse with him in several languages; and I found him master of all those that I could speak. I conversed with him five or six hours together in Arabic. He told me there was scarce a true history to be found. I asked him what he thought of Mahomet, the Prophet and Lawgiver of the Mussulmans? He answered that he knew his father very well, and had often been in his company at Ormus in Persia; that Mahomet was a man full of light and a divine spirit, but had his errors as well as other mortals, and that his chiefest was in denying the crucifixion of the Messias; 'for,' said he, 'I was present, and saw Him hang on the Cross, with these eyes of mine.' He accused the Mussulmans of 'imposture' in making the world believe that the tomb of their Prophet hangs miraculously between heaven and earth, saying that he himself had seen it, and that it was built after the manner of other sepulchres. Thou who hast been at the Holy Place knowest whether this be true or false. He upbraids the Persian Mahometans with luxury, the Ottomans with tyranny, the Arabians with robbery, the Moors with cruelty, and the Mussulmans of the Indies with atheism. Nor does he spare to reproach the Christian churches: he taxes the Roman and Grecian with the pompous idolatry of heathens; he accuses the Æthiopian of Judaism, the Armenian of heresy; and says that the Protestants, if they would live according to their profession, would be the best Christians.

"He told me he was in Rome when Nero set fire to the city and stood triumphing on the top of a hill to behold the flames. That he saw Saladin's return from his conquests in the East, when he caused his shirt to be carried on the top of a spear, with his proclamation: *'Saladin, lord of many rich countries, Conqueror of the East,* ever victorious and happy, when he dies shall have no other memorial left of all his glories, but only this poor shirt.'

"He relates many remarkable passages of Soliman the Magnificent, whereof our histories are silent, and says he was in Constantinople when Soliman built that royal mosque which goes by his name. He knew Tamerlane the Scythian, and told me he was so called because he halted on one leg. He pretends also to have been acquainted with Scander-Beg, the valiant and fortunate Prince of Epirus. He seemed to pity the insupportable calamity of Bajazet, whom he had seen carried about in a cage by Tamerlane's order. He accuses the Scythian of too barbarous an insult on the unfortunate Sultan. He remembers the ancient Caliphs of Babylon and Egypt, the empire of the Saracens, and the wars in the Holy Land. He highly extols the valour and conduct of the renowned Godfrey de Bouillon. He gives an accurate account of the rise, progress, establishment and subversion of the Mamelukes in Egypt. He says he has washed himself in the two headsprings of the river Nile, which arise in the southern part of Æthiopia. That its increase is occasioned by the great rains in Æthiopia, which swell all the rivers that fall into the Nile, and cause that vast inundation to discover whose origin has so much puzzled philosophy. He says the river Ganges in India is broader and deeper than the Nile; that the river Niger in Africa is longer by some hundreds of miles; and that he can remember a time when the river Nile overflowed not till three months after the usual season.

"Having professed himself an universal traveller, and that there was no corner of the earth where he had not been present, I began to comfort myself with the hopes of some news from the Ten Tribes of Israel that were carried into captivity by Salmanasar, King of Assyria, and could never be heard of since. I asked him several questions concerning them, but found no satisfactory answer. Only, he told me that in Asia, Africa, and Europe he had taken notice of a sort of people who (though not Jews by profession) yet retained some characteristics whereby one might discover them to be descended of that nation. In Livonia, Russia, and Finland he had met with people of languages distinct from that of the country, having a great mixture of Hebrew words; that these abstained from swine's flesh, blood, and things strangled; that in their lamentations for the dead they always used these words: *Jeru, Jeru, Masco, Salem.* By which, he thought, they called to remembrance Jerusalem and Damascus, those two famous cities of Palestine and Syria. In the Circassians also he had traced some footsteps of Judaism: their customs, manner of life, feasts, marriages, and scarifices being not far removed from the institutions of Mosaic Law. But, what is most remarkable, he said that he had conversed with professed Jews in the north part of Asia who never so much as heard of Jesus, the son of Mary, or of the revolutions of Judea after his death, the siege and destruction of Jerusalem, or any other matters wherewith all histories abound concerning that nation. He said, moreover, that these Jews had only the Pentateuch, not having heard of the rest of those Books which compose the greatest part of the Old Testament; and that this Pentateuch was written in a sort of Hebrew far different from that which is now commonly spoken by the rest of the Jews dispersed throughout the world. That the number of these Jews was infinite. And, finally, he thought that these (if any) were the true posterity of those Ten Captive Tribes.

"Having mentioned the destruction of Jerusalem, I asked him where he was at that time? He told me, in the Court of Vespasian at Rome; and that he had heard the emperor say, when he understood the Temple of Solomon was burnt to ashes, 'he had rather all Rome had been set on fire.' Here the old man fell a-weeping himself, lamenting the ruin of that noble structure, which he described to me as familiarly as if he had seen it but yesterday. He says that Josephus wrote partially of the seditions in the city, being related to one of the chief ringleaders, whom therefore he spared, being loth to stain the reputation of his own family to all posterity.

"I tell thee, sage Cheik, if this man's pretences be true, he is so full of choice memoirs, and has been witness to so many grand transactions for the space of sixteen centuries of years, that he may not unfitly be called 'A Living Chronology,' the 'Protonotary of the Christians' Hegira', or principal recorder of that which they esteem the last *epocha* of the world's duration. By his looks one would take him for a relic of the Old World, or one of the long-lived fathers before the Flood. To speak modestly, he may pass for the younger brother of Time.

"It would be endless to tell thee how many other discourses we had of his travels and memoirs; till, tired with his company, and judging all to be a cheat, I took my leave. I assure thee, he seems to be a man well versed in all histories, a great traveller, and one that affects to be counted an extraordinary person. The common people are ready to adore him; and the very fear of the multitude restrains the magistrates from offering any violence to this impostor.

"Live though in the exercise of thy reason, which will not permit thee to be seduced into errors by the subtle insinuations of men. Continue to love Mahomet, who honours thee without a fiction."

10. The Wandering Jew in England

THE Legend of the Wandering Jew had been known in England, and different versions had arisen in Ireland, in Scotland and in the English rural areas. But it was not until the middle of the seventeenth century that an appearance in England of the Wanderer was reported.

A man named Samuel Wallis, who lived in Stamford, reported in 1658 that the Wandering Jew had appeared to him at his home, though no one else had seen him.

It happened on a Sunday evening when Wallis, a man suffering from the late stages of tuberculosis, sat before the hearth in his invalid's chair, engrossed in a book. Suddenly he heard a knock on the door. Since he was alone in the house, Wallis made his way to the door with great effort and opened it. In the doorway stood a tall, grave old man, dressed in a purple coat buttoned down to the waist, new-looking breeches of the same color, and in stockings of a gleaming white. The color of his walking stick too was white as was his beard and the hair on his head. Though it had rained all day, there was not a speck on his clothes or mud on his shoes.

While Wallis was observing him, the stranger said in a pleasant voice: "Friend, I pray thee give an old pilgrim a cup of small beere!"

Samuel Wallis bid him welcome and served him beer. When the stranger finished drinking, he said, "Friend, thou art not well?" Wallis explained he had been ill for many years, and the doctors had told him he was past curing.

"By the help and power of Almighty God above, thou shalt be well," said the stranger. And he gave Wallis a *recipe* of "two leaves of red sage and one of bloodworte," to be taken daily with his beer. Then the stranger departed.

Samuel Wallis followed the stranger's prescription and soon became well. And when his story became known, the divines of Stamford debated long and heatedly whether the stranger was an angel or a devil.

Toward the end of the seventeenth century a man appeared in England who called himself the Wandering Jew, and created a sensation. He was listened to by the ignorant and gullible, but called an "impostor" by the educated. Curiously enough, members of the nobility seem to have taken notice of him, and their attention gave him a prestige he would not otherwise have commanded. Partly in jest, partly out of curiosity, but partly also out of the boredom that afflicts that class, they arranged gatherings of distinguished guests, at which the Wanderer entertained them by answering outlandish questions about the past.

The Wanderer, calling himself Ahasuerus, answered all questions; and the more remote the past into which the inquiries delved, the greater his confidence, and the greater the amusement of his audience.

He declared to them that in the days of Jesus he had been an officer of the Sanhedrin, and never a shoemaker, cordwainer, mechanic, or guard in Pilate's court, as had been erroneously reported. He recalled all the Apostles and described their appearance, their clothes, and their personal peculiarities, often correcting descriptions given of them in apocryphal documents.

He spoke in many languages, which he claimed to have learned during the centuries he had roamed over the earth. And he also claimed the power of healing, provided that the sick who came to him had complete faith in his healing powers.

His hosts soon decided that, whoever he might actually be, he was a person of wide knowledge and personal magnetism, and that if he was acting the part, he was a superb actor. He could talk to them with a humility that humbled them. He never smiled or engaged in trivial conversation. He was abstemious. And if he accepted a gift, he accepted it with the manner of one conferring a favor upon the donor. The things he did and the things he said were repeated in high and low places. And invitations came to him from Oxford and Cambridge that the professors might question him there.

When the professors of both institutions of learning found discrepancies between his historical accounts and those recorded in the history books, Ahasuerus maintained that most of the history books were not to be relied upon because they were written to prove one nation or another right or wrong; and he could quote from historians of different and opposing nationalities who presented the same historic event quite differently.

One English nobleman questioned him in Arabic concerning Mohammed. And Ahasuerus replied in Arabic that he had known young Abdallah, Mohammed's father, though Mohammed had not known his own father who had died before Mohammed was born. He also knew Mohammed's grandfather, Abd-al-Muttalib, who reared the grandson in Mecca until he was eight years old. But on his next visit, several years later, he found that Abd-al-Muttalib had died and Mohammed had gone to live with his uncle, abu Talib. These and many other things the stranger remembered of Mohammed's family, and of the times when Mohammed gathered thousands under the Green Banner and went out to convert people to Islam.

Ahasuerus related an incident about Mohammed, whom he considered a very intelligent and just leader. Mohammed had expressed the opinion that Jesus did not die at the Crucifixion. "I told him," said the stranger, "that he was in error, for I was a witness to the truth of that event."

He was questioned about Nero, and asked whether it was true that he had set fire to Rome; he was questioned about Saladin, the Kurdish-Moslem leader of the twelfth century who led the campaign against the third Crusade; he was interrogated about Timur Lenk (Timur the Lame), who became known as Tamerlane. The stranger recalled an incident of his personal involvement in an event in Angora, which brought him face to face with this cruel conqueror who claimed to be a descendant of Genghis Khan. He was asked about Bajazet I, the Ottoman sultan whom Tamerlane defeated in battle and carried in an iron cage after routing the Sultan near Angora. The stranger did not know him, but he had met Bajazet II, who was much less concerned with warfare

and much more with the culture of his people and the re-
building of Constantinople, which had been devastated
by an earthquake.

Questions were put to him about many other people
and events in history, and on most of them he had much
to say. He asserted he had been there when the events
were happening, and, knowing he was deathless, he could
dare to enter into areas too dangerous for ordinary
mortals.

What happened to this stranger, who insisted he was
the one and only Wandering Jew, is nowhere told. He
disappeared from London as he had appeared, without
warning; and was next heard of as having been seen in
Denmark.

We find echoes of this visit of the Wandering Jew to
England in English pamphlets, and in fiction of a much
later date.

The incident of the cross-examination at Oxford is
used in a book (on which we will have more to say
later on) entitled *My First Two Thousand Years: The
Autobiography of the Wandering Jew*. Authors Viereck
and Eldrige give a description of their hero, Isaac
Laquedem, the true Wandering Jew, and his constant
companion Kotikokura, accidentally witnessing the cross-
examination at Oxford of an impostor claiming to be
Ahasuerus the Wandering Jew. The impostor answers the
questions of the Oxford dons and a bishop on diverse
historical matters, and in several languages, and is on
the point of convincing all those who had gathered to
question him and the large audience of students and professors who had come to listen.

Finally, when almost everyone's doubts seem to have
melted away, Isaac Laquedem, the true Wandering Jew
and the only one who can really weigh the accuracy of
the answers, bombards Ahasuerus with questions that
reach their mark like well-aimed poisoned arrows, and
the impostor crumples, exposed as a fraud. For the man
does not know his own father's name, or that of his

mother. To which Isaac Laquedem adds that the impostor's pretended poverty is the greatest fraud of all, for the Eternal Jew is "wealthier than kings."

Isaac Laquedem later records: "My familiarity with the story of the Wandering Jew aroused suspicion. The Oxford professors attempted to entrap me in divers discussions. It tested my ingenuity to escape from the meshes of their cross-examination. I was not in a mood to play with danger, and shook the dust of Oxford off my heels leaving behind me a pair of boots."

Later, browsing in a London bookshop, Isaac comes across a pamphlet in Latin entitled: *The Wandering Jew—His Trial at Oxford University, His Remarks, Opinions and Ideas Expounded, Commented Upon and Analyzed by the Reverend Bishop of Canterbury with annotations by Master Aubrey and Master Battermann, Doctors of Sacred Theology.*

During the early part of the nineteenth century, at intervals of several years, there were reports of mysterious strangers claiming to be the Wandering Jew. These men were called impostors by some, and demented by others. And some, believing, listened to these men with fear and pity. But in these late appearances nothing memorable happened to preserve the reports as other than vague rumors. The last appearance of such a person in England was recorded in 1830.

11. The Wandering Jew Among the Slavs

THE Legend of the Wandering Jew had at an early date traveled across Europe into the Slavic countries where it became deeply rooted. The Deathless Old Man,

as he was often called in Eastern Europe, was reported
seen in many towns and cities, from Belgrade to Saratov
and from Warsaw to Moscow. As the legend traveled
orally eastward, though it remained the same in essence,
it took on details which reflected the Slavonic tempera-
ment.

For many centuries, and to the present day in countries where the legend still survives, the Wandering Jew
was principally an oral tradition. But written accounts
of the legend in Slovenian, Polish, Lithuanian,
Ruthenian and Russian folklore are quite extensive,
though few of them are available in English translation.
The Eastern legends of the Wanderer are repetitions of
the legends told elsewhere, with occasional interesting
variations.

Some of the Slavic variations concern the Wanderer's
age and his mode of penitence.

When the moon is young, according to one legend,
the Wandering Jew appears young, and when the moon is
old, he appears old. In this version, obviously, the Wandering Jew is in some way equated with the Man in the
Moon, about whom there are many folk legends.

A number of Slavic legends begin with a fixed form of
interrogation of the Wanderer when he appears. He is
asked, "When did you arrive here?" He invariably replies to that, "Yesterday." And when asked "When will
you leave?" he invariably replies, "Tomorrow."

In one Slavic legend the cobbler had pushed Jesus in
front of his shop and urged Him to move on, but immediately repented his deed. He ran to the grave of his
young daughter to confess his sin. But his child came out
of the grave and cried: "Faithless father! You are faithless toward God and do not deserve to receive solace on
my grave!" And the broken-hearted father left her grave
and began to wander from place to place. He wanders
over the entire world, but can find no peace, and he must
continue to wander disconsolate and heartbroken. When
the moon is in its last quarter, he turns ashen-gray and

feeble; his face becomes wrinkled and his hands tremble; and his matted gray hair reaches down to his shoulders. But when the moon is new, he grows young and strong, straight as a cedar, his features glowing with health, his hair raven-black, his eyes full of passion. And women are warned against his charms.

In other legends the Wanderer not only changes from age to youth and from youth to old age with the changes in the moon, but he is also capable of changing himself at will into a dog or other domestic animal or beast of burden, which he does from time to time as acts of penance.

One legend presents the Wandering Jew as a man who had pondered upon his fate for centuries, and then suddenly experienced a change of heart and a great conversion. Though he remained the same physically, in his heart he then knew that his fate was not a curse, but an act of Christian charity. For though he was still an alien in the world and destined to wander, he was destined to wander with the mission of love for life and for mankind, and to teach others the brotherhood of man. In this legend he appears only to people who need him. He appears, in particular, to people in great despair who are contemplating suicide, and he convinces them of the duty of every man to live out his destiny, despite all difficulties. To such a person he relates the story of his own life of loneliness and wandering, and by his own example he succeeds in persuading these desperate people that there is hope for all.

Among the Slavic legends there are some which relate that two men were cursed for the sin of driving Jesus on when He stopped to rest, and cursed, not to wander, but to wait unceasingly outside His sepulcher, until He comes again.

12. The Wandering Jew Among the Mormons

LONG after an appearance of the Wandering Jew is last reported anywhere in Europe—and when the legend had long since become the basis for allegorical poems, romantic novels, and symbolical dramas—there was a report of his spectacular appearance in America. And the legend, in modified form, thrived and still thrives in Mormon lore. The theory has been advanced, with considerable plausibility, that the Legend of the Wandering Jew (along with other legends about immortals) has been absorbed and transformed by the Mormons into the Legend of the Three Nephites, who bear many points of resemblance and are sometimes even confused with the Wandering Jew.

The Three Nephites almost invariably appear singly but have identical characteristics, their true names are unknown, and to the people to whom they become manifest they seem one person. Like the Wandering Jew, the Nephite appears as an old, white-haired man, wearing ancient clothes, and claiming to have known no rest since the days of Jesus; and, like the Wandering Jew, the Nephite is fated not to taste death until the Second Coming. But whereas the Wandering Jew was cursed not to taste death until Judgment Day for the sin he had committed, the Three Nephites, like John the Beloved Disciple, were blessed not to taste death because they were saintly disciples of Jesus.

To understand how the Three Nephites came into being, and how the *Buttadeus* (the God Smiter) was transformed, in Mormon lore, into the *Espera en Dios*

(Hope in God), one must go to the Mormon Scriptures.

According to The Book of Mormon, which covers a period of more than a thousand years—from 599 B.C. to A.D. 421, there lived in Jerusalem in the days of King Zedekiah (599 B.C. in Biblical chronology) a righteous man named Lehi, who was a direct descendant of Joseph, son of Jacob. Lehi was among the prophets of his day who prophesied the destruction of Jerusalem because of the wickedness of its inhabitants, and when the people heard his prophecies, they sought to kill him. Then the Lord commanded Lehi to take his wife Sariah and his four sons, Laman, Lemuel, Sam and Nephi, and go into the wilderness. After many trials and afflictions, they migrated by a boat of their own making to the Promised Land (South America). And there the descendants of Lehi split into two groups: the Lamanites, offspring of Lehi's oldest son, who became wicked, and for their sinful ways were cursed with red skins (and became the ancestors of the American Indians); and the Nephites, offspring of Lehi's youngest son who were "white and delightful people." And in the Promised Land the Lamanites and the Nephites lived for several centuries.

Now, after the Crucifixion and the Resurrection of Jesus and the establishment of His church at Jerusalem, He came to the Nephites of South America and established His church in the New World. During his stay with the Nephites he chose twelve apostles to carry out His work. They were, according to The Book of Mormon: Nephi; Timothy, his brother; Jonas, Timothy's son; Mathoni; Mathonihah, his brother; Kumen; Kumenonthi; Jonas; Zedekiah; and Isaiah. (III Nephi 19:4) Jesus called these twelve together and gave them instructions about their respective missions in the New World.

"And it came to pass when Jesus had said these words, he spake unto his disciples, one by one, saying unto them 'What is it that ye desire of me, after that I am gone to the Father?' " Nine of the twelve asked that after their mission was accomplished they be permitted to die. And Jesus said to them, "Blessed are ye because ye desire this thing of me: therefore, after ye are seventy-and-two years old ye shall come unto me in my kingdom; and with me ye shall find rest." But the other three dared not speak their wish, and Jesus knowing what was in their minds, said, "Behold, I know your thoughts, as ye have desired the thing with John, my beloved, who was with me in my ministry, before that I was lifted up by the Jews, desired of me. Therefore, more blessed are ye, for ye shall never taste of death; but shall live to behold all the doings of the Father unto the children of men, even until all things shall be fulfilled according to the will of the Father, when I shall come in my glory with the powers of heaven. And ye shall never endure the pains of death; but when I shall come in my glory ye shall be changed in the twinkling of an eye from mortality to immortality."

All this was recorded on indestructable plates by Mormon, "A pure descendant of Lehi," who, in the same chapter (III Nephi 28) adds: "Behold, I was about to write the names of th   were never to taste of death, but the Lord forbade; therefore I write them not, and they are hid from the world."

In A.D. 421 the son of Mormon, Moroni, completed the record begun by Nephi and carried forward by his father. He sealed the record, and it was hidden from the world until the night of September 21, 1823, when Moroni came to Joseph Smith, who then lived in Palmyra, New York, and told him of the plates "giving an account of the former inhabitants of this continent, and the source from whence they sprang." Four years later, on September 22, 1827, the plates were revealed to him. By the gift of the power of God, The Book of Mormon was translated into modern speech and first published in 1830.

Joseph Smith, to whom The Book of Mormon was revealed, may have been familiar with the European legends of the Wandering Jew, for the legend was well known in New England during the early part of the nineteenth century. Certainly some of the early German and English converts to Mormonism, who brought the Legend of the Wandering Jew to Utah, must have invested it with spiritual meaning after reading the Books of Nephi in The Book of Mormon. And slowly the legend was transformed until it became part of the religious lore of the Mormon Church.

The appearance of one of the Three Nephites (sometimes confused with the Wandering Jew) has been reported frequently in Utah. "Stories about the Three Nephites run into the hundreds," writes the American folklorist, Dr. Wayland D. Hand (*Southern Folklore Quarterly,* September, 1938). They appeared to heal people, to help them in their hour of need, to bless them for their hospitality, and, principally, to bring a message to their hosts about the truth of the Gospel.

In a Mormon publication in Salt Lake City, the *Juvenile Instructor,* an article appeared serially in 1886, entitled *A Mysterious Preacher* by one Hyrum Belnap, which resembles in many respects the stories told about the Wandering Jew—particularly in Slavic lore. Here is the story as summarized by Dr. Hand:

"On a calm, sunny day in May, 1878, a clap of thunder resounded over the city of Lexington, Henderson County, Tennessee. The sound was heard distinctly for eight miles around and subsequent reports indicated that it had been heard as far as thirty miles. This phenomenon aroused much curiosity, since there was not a cloud in the sky and there was no storm after the thunder. On the afternoon of the same day there appeared near Lexington, the county seat, a strange man, of spare build, medium height, fair skin, dark brown curly hair, and a light beard of reddish cast. He was poorly clad. His appearance indicated that he was about thirty years of age. He announced a religious meeting to be held in the neighborhood that evening. Because of the unusual nature of his arrival, his apparent knowledge of the roads and even paths in the fields, the meeting was well attended. He conducted the meeting alone, sang and preached in a manner unlike that of evangelistic preaching current at the time. At the conclusion of the meeting, when plied with questions, he said that his name was Robert Edge, and that he belonged to the Church of God. He refused to reveal whence he had come. At the solicitation of the congregation he appointed other meetings to be held in the vicinity, and soon his fame as a preacher had spread far and near. In due time, by an exchange of notes and gossip, it was discovered that no one had ever seen him any distance from a place of worship, and that he was never seen until he arrived in the crowd or had assumed his place in the pulpit. Persons appointed to watch him lost track of him before he had proceeded far. He never inquired directions from one place to another, and yet always arrived according to appointment. A case in point: At the close of a certain meeting a stranger asked Mr. Edge to speak at his house six miles distant the following Wednesday. The preacher accepted but, to the surprise of the host, did not ask him, nor anyone else, directions to his home. As usual he arrived at the appointed hour.

"In his subsequent preaching Mr. Edge made allegations and attacks on various churches that brought him the ill will of many of his congregation and the animosity of the clergy. It was soon rumored that he might be a Mormon preacher. This he would neither confirm or deny. More determined than ever to find out who he was, they commissioned one Jones, a Baptist deacon, to find out the truth. Jones went to a house where Mr. Edge had eaten and proceeded at once to interrogate him.

Mr. Jones: "My friend, where are you from?"
Mr. Edge: "From about six miles."
Mr. Jones: "What church do you belong to?"
Mr. Edge: "The Church of God, sir."

Mr. Jones:	"Where is it?"
Mr. Edge:	"In the United States."
Mr. Jones:	"You have been speaking about one being ordained before he had the right to preach. By whom were you ordained?"
Mr. Edge:	"By Jesus Christ, sir."
Mr. Jones:	"Where?"
Mr. Edge:	"In Eternity."
Mr. Jones:	"How long have you been preaching?"
Mr. Edge:	"About eighteen hundred years."

" 'At this point,' Belnap's article reads, 'Mr. Jones sprang to his feet and walked away in disgust.' "

"Mr. Edge gathered around himself a little flock of adherents, performed a number of healings, married couples and imposed his hands in blessings, but would not baptize the people."

After Robert Edge disappeared (and some said that he had left for England to carry on the good work), many stories began to circulate about him. Some claimed he was one of the Three Nephites. But others argued that since his appearance had been heralded by miraculous thunder, and since he refused to baptize people, he must have been the Wandering Jew.

Then one day, as they leafed through a Bible which belonged to one Sireneous Reed, they discovered Edge's signature directly under the passage: *And he shall send his angels with a great sound of a trumpet, and they shall gather together his elect from the four winds* (Matthew 24:31).

This revealed to them who he really was, though his name remained hidden by the command of God.

Sometimes one of the Nephites appeared in a community or a household, visible to some but invisible to others; or he would be visible to men and invisible to animals, particularly horses who would have run over the stranger if their masters had not pulled in the reins in time. Often the Nephite would appear miraculously, without leaving any tracks in the newly fallen snow outside the door when coming or when leaving.

Though the Nephites almost invariably made their appearance singly, there is on record one occasion when all Three were seen together, and that was the time that they appeared to the archer of Christopher Columbus.

In *The Life and Voyages of Christopher Columbus,* Washington Irving records that during Columbus's second voyage to the Americas, he dropped anchor along the coast of Cuba near a beautiful palm grove. "Here [Irving goes on] a party was sent on shore for wood and water, and found two living springs in the midst of the grove. While they were employed in cutting wood and filling their water casks, an archer strayed into the forest with his cross-bow in search of game, but soon returned, flying with great terror, and calling loudly his companions for aid. He declared that he had not proceeded far, when he suddenly espied through an opening glade, a man in a long white dress so like a friar of the order of St. Mary of Mercy, that at first sight he took him for the chaplain of the admiral. Two others followed in white tunics reaching to their knees, and the three were fair complexioned, as Europeans."

Upon this report Columbus sent two expeditions inland in search of the three white men, but both parties returned without finding any trace of them. Washington Irving apologizes for recording the episode, since no tribe of Indians in Cuba was ever found who wore clothing, and the archer's report was either an error or a falsehood. But Professor E. D. Partridge of Brigham Young University, in his diligent search for evidence of the divine origin of The Book of Mormon, is convinced that what the archer saw was an assembly of the Three Nephites.

Among the numerous stories of the appearances of the Three Nephites still current in Utah today, two are of particular interest to us because they are clearly about the Wandering Jew.

In 1939 Mr. A. E. Fife and his wife went out to collect oral versions of the Legend of the Three Nephites current in southwestern Utah. In St. George they interviewed an old man of ninety-three, Charles Seegmiller, a German by birth, who recalled an event which took place when he was a young man of twenty-four. The Fifes recorded his story as he told it:

"There was surely a queer incident of that character down on the Muddy here. My brothers Adam and Billy was there—it was before I went down there. One day they was settin' around—kind of a windy day—and all at once they seen a man comin' along the desert. This desert was a plateau above the Muddy Valley, on the east of the Valley, and it was just only covered with evergreens, green bushes, so you could see all over. Well, this man, he come, and they was choppin' some wood there.

"He said, 'How to do,' and waited a few minutes and said, 'I would like if you would let me have some dry bread and some patches to patch my clothes,' and he says, 'I am goin' to cross the desert here and I would like to have somet'ing of that kind.'

"My brother Billy looked at him and said, 'Do you know what kind o' country you are goin' over? I don't see that you've got much preparation. I've been over that country lots of times and you haven't hardly got anyt'ing to pack water with.'

"He says, 'Oh, yes, but I know how to get water.'

"Then they says to him, 'What do you want dry bread for? We'll give you some good bread to go over there.'

" 'No, I want dry bread, if you got it. Good bread sometimes spoils, but dry bread won't spoil.'

"They talked and finally he says, 'I'll be goin' soon.'

"They says, 'Well, what might your name be?'

"So he talked German to them: 'Man heisst mich der ewige Jude [They call me the eternal Jew].'

"Well, they paid no attention to it, but when he got away it come to them, 'Well, that must be the rovin' Jew.'

"It was about as far from here to the Temple [Saint George Temple, about eight blocks from Mr. Seegmiller's home], to a drop off the valley. Everyt'ing was clear, and he couldn't make that distance in the time since he left them. They run out to look for him but they couldn't see him anywhere.

"I've often wondered why they didn't follow his tracks."

In this incident as recounted in the *Journal of American Folklore,* the old man, Seegmiller, definitely identified the mysterious visitor as the Eternal Jew (using the German designation for the Wandering Jew).

An even more positive identification of the Wandering Jew appearing on the American scene is made in an editorial in *The Desert News* of Salt Lake City, dated Wednesday, September 23, 1868.

"Quite an excitement, it is reported, was recently caused in the village of Harts Corners, a few miles from New York, by the appearance of the veritable 'Wandering Jew.' Now an ordinary wandering Jew would not be at all likely to create any surprise, seeing that they are to be met with in every quarter; but the case would be quite contrary—even in a community of beer and tobacco loving Dutchmen, the very embodiment of all that is imperturbable, if the genuine Ahasuerus—condemned by the Great Teacher to walk the earth until the day of judgment—were to make his appearance in their midst. So nobody can wonder at the excitement displayed by the people of Harts Corners on the appearance of this very notorious and venerable character in their midst!

"The discovery was made under the following circumstances: On the second instant, as two little boys were going a fishing, their attention was arrested by deep groans, which seemed to emanate from an old shanty they passed on their way. The boys entered the shanty and there beheld a venerable looking individual with a long white beard, dressed in black flowing garments, seated in one corner, apparently in pain. They manifested a desire to assist him, but were frightened off by the old man lifting his staff in a threatening manner. The youngsters retreated and soon returned with a number of the villagers, who, on entering the shanty saw an individual with a large hooked nose, larger ears, and finger nails about an inch long—there was no tail visible at least. They asked what ailed him, and he replied that he had fallen on a stone and severely hurt his leg. In the course of conversation he also informed them that he had no home, and his last friend had departed this life long before the light of heaven illumined the soul of any amongst them, and the voice of the only one he loved was silent in the tomb before printing was invented, or America had ever echoed to the cry of liberty.

"Exclamations of 'cracked' escaped several of the crowd, which aroused the indignation of the Jew, who asked them why they came there if they did not believe him. They replied they came because they had heard there was a man in trouble and they wished to assist him. To this he replied 'man *can* not and Heaven *will* not.' He then gave a short account of his recent travels from Siberia to America *via* Behring Straits, through the wilds of Alaska, etc., saying the first kind word he had heard during the whole journey was from the party he was then addressing. He then bade them adieu and departed.

"In his hasty departure on this occasion, as he is said to have done on many others, he left a memento by which his identity was fully proven. This time it was an old volume of extracts from the Babylonian Talmud, in the Hebrew character. On a fly leaf was a short account of his birth, parentage, the sentence of the Savior and his subsequent wanderings, all clearly proving that he was the identical *bona fide* Wandering Jew. This remarkable book, proving the identity of poor Ahasuerus, is now in the possession of one Michael O'Grady, a switch tender and farmer living a short distance from the place where the Jew was discovered. By applying to him, any one sufficiently interested may doubtless obtain further details in relation to this—the very 'last sensation'; of course they may!"

Appearances of one of the Three Nephites have been reported in rural Utah until very recently; but the last appearances of the Wandering Jew seem to be those two American appearances: one in Harts Corner, New York, in 1868, as reported in *The Desert News*; and the other in Muddy Valley, Utah, in 1870, as described by the old man, Charles Seegmiller.

Before that time, and since, the legend has inspired poems, novels and dramas, some of which enjoyed incredible popularity—indicating that the Wandering Jew, or the symbol he represents, still lingers in folk imagination the world over.

But before we discuss the literature based on the legend, let us first examine some of the roots of the legend and see how deeply they reach into man's consciousness.

Part Two

ROOTS OF THE
LEGEND

*"As a myth, its roots lie in that great
mystery of human life which is an
enigma never solved, and ever originating
speculation."*

—S.
BARING-GOULD

1. Bible Sources

THE Legend of the Wandering Jew, from a Christian point of view, is deeply inconsistent and disconcerting. For it ascribes to Jesus—in the hour when He was about to die for all sinners—the pronouncement of a curse upon a sinner who rejected and maltreated him. And it was inevitable that the Bible would be examined for any statement that could be interpreted as foreshadowing proof of the literal existence of the Wandering Jew and that would place the legend beyond refutation or regret.

THE NEW TESTAMENT QUOTATIONS

Since the fate of the Wanderer was determined by a pronouncement by Jesus, the first authority searched was the New Testament. And the search was rewarding: not only one but several passages were found which, as interpreted by imaginative commentators and exegetes, justified the belief in the literal existence of the Wandering Jew.

To begin with, there is the passage in Matthew (understood by the imperative clause, *Verily I say unto you*) in which Jesus has foretold his own death and admonished those who would follow him to bear the Cross, which ends with: *Verily I say unto you, There be some standing here, which shall not taste of death, till they see the Son of man coming in his kingdom* (16:28).

Here we have a statement upon which the concept of

the Three Nephites might have been founded, as well as all Christian legends of people blessed or cursed not to *taste of death, till* the Second Coming.

Ten chapters later in Matthew—when Jesus tells his disciples that one of them will betray Him—He says: *The Son of man goeth as it is written of him: but woe unto that man by whom the Son of man is betrayed! it had been good for that man if he had not been born* (26:24). And farther on in the same chapter we find another stave, so to speak, of which legends are made. This is the chapter of the Betrayal, in which Judas appears leading a multitude with swords and staves. *Then came they, and laid hands on Jesus, and took him. And, behold, one of them which were with Jesus stretched out his hand, and drew his sword, and struck a servant of the high priest's, and smote off his ear* (26:50-51).

These last two passages in Matthew have been interpreted as proof that the Wandering Jew is Judas *by whom the Son of man is betrayed;* others have argued that the Wanderer is the man named as *a servant of the high priest's.* And, in either case, *it had been good for that man if he had not been born.*

In the Gospels, Judas is invariably identified as Judas Iscariot, *who also betrayed Him,* to distinguish him from the Disciple Judas who was the brother of James. But the early Christian Gnostics wanted to know how such a one as Judas Iscariot could have been chosen as a Disciple by Jesus, and allowed to enjoy the grace of the Apostolate. How could Jesus, who had divine wisdom, have allowed him among his Disciples, they asked. And their view was that Judas acted as he did out of the sincere conviction that Jesus was the Son of God, that he fully believed that when the attempt was made to crucify Him, mankind would be instantly redeemed. The sin of Judas, they argued, was not that he lacked faith, but that he acted to hasten the moment. And they claimed that was why Judas was cursed not to *taste of death* and to wander in perpetual penance and atonement till the Second Coming.

In Mark there is a repetition and confirmation of the two passages in Matthew (16:28 and 26:50-51) with slight variations (Mark 9:1 and 14:46-7). In Luke we find a confirmation of Matthew and Mark in their statements that Jesus foretold, *There be some standing here, which shall not taste of death, till they see the kingdom of God* (Luke 9:27).

But in John additional and new material was found upon which the Legend of the Wandering Jew could be more securely established. In the episode of the arrest, John names the Disciple who drew the sword and cut off the ear of the High Priest's servant as Simon Peter; and he names the maimed servant as Malchus (John 18:10). Later on in the same chapter, John relates another incident that may have served as the foundation of the legend. He relates that when Jesus was interrogated by the High Priest, He answers that He had never spoken in secret but had preached in the synagogue and in the temple, and that everyone knew what He said. *And when he had thus spoken, one of the officers which stood by struck Jesus with the palm of his hand, saying, Answerest thou the high priest so? Jesus answered him, If I have spoken evil, bear witness of the evil: but if well, why smitest thou me?* (18:22-3). Though the name of the officer is not given, it is undoubtedly he who was later called "Buttadeus"—the God Smiter.

In addition to the passages on Malchus (whom John named) and on the officer who struck Jesus at the interrogation before the High Priest (whom John does not name) there is still another passage in which John records the maltreatment of Jesus by other Roman soldiers. *And the soldiers platted a crown of thorns, and put it on his head, and they put on him a purple robe, And said, Hail, King of the Jews! and they smote him with their hands* (19:2-3). From this passage may have come the legendary Cartaphilus who, as we have seen, dominated all the early legends about the doomed Wanderer.

These citations from the New Testament, taken collectively, yielded the basis for the christological legend of a soldier in Pilate's court, doomed to wander over the earth until Judgment Day. Other passages in the Bible yielded the basic material for other legends about men who were not to *taste of death,* which, in turn, became interwoven into the legend of what later evolved as the Repentant Wanderer or Eternal Jew.

In time the legend became refined into a universal symbol which conveyed man's preoccupation with the enigma of death and the search for redemption. But the concept of men blessed or cursed not to *taste of death* had already appeared in the Old Testament.

And those who searched the Old Testament for further assurances that men could, by the will of God, become immortal, or that God would condemn some men to eternal wandering for a great sin they had committed soon found corroboration of what they had hoped to find.

CAIN THE WANDERER

The first wanderer to appear in the Bible is Adam's son, Cain. Early in Genesis we come upon the story of Cain and Abel. For the murder committed by Cain, God denounces him, saying: *And now* art *thou cursed from the earth, which hath opened her mouth to receive thy brother's blood from thy hand . . . a fugitive and a vagabond shalt thou be in the earth.* And later *the Lord set a mark upon Cain, lest any finding him should kill him* (Genesis 4:11-15).

The mark God set upon Cain, according to the *Midrash Rabbah* (The Great commentary of the Bible), was the letter *C,* so that all who met him might know that he was the first man to have committed fratricide, and also to warn them not to harm him, since Cain was responsible for his crime to God only. Cain, the commentary goes on, was driven from the East of the Garden of

Eden; but wherever he went, there storms arose; the ground his feet touched shook and quaked; and all living creatures ran from him in fear. Then Cain complained to the Lord: "Yesterday you banished my father Adam from the Garden of Eden; today you banished me to become a wanderer. It will soon be said that the only punishment You can mete out is banishment!" God relented and took him to the Land of Nod—the Land of the Wanderer, far to the East of Eden, and there He allowed him to remain as a fugitive; and He ordered the earth to be still, and the animals neither to fear nor harm Cain.

A number of versions of the Legend of the Wandering Jew show marked similarity to the Legend of Cain the Wanderer. And in some versions of the legend the Wandering Jew is identified as Cain; and we are told that the Wanderer can be recognized by the mark on his forehead—a flaming cross that consumes his brain as fast as it is renewed. The mark on his forehead is his shame and sorrow; and he keeps his forehead covered and does not let anyone see it. In these legends no one can hurt or harm the Wanderer with impunity, since he is responsible for his great sin only to the Lord.

THE UNDYING ENOCH

The concepts of longevity, and immortality, are also given early in the Old Testament. Soon after the story of Cain the record of the preflood, long-lived generation is presented. Among them we find Jared, Enoch's father, who lived nine hundred and sixty-two years; and Methuselah, Enoch's son, who lived seven years longer than his grandfather. But Enoch, a righteous man, and the first pre-Abrahamite recorded as a believer in one God, lived a mere three hundred and sixty-five years— one year for every day in the year—and then, because he was favored by God, *he* was *not; for God took him* (Genesis 5:24).

In this instance a man was not allowed to *taste of death* because of his righteousness. And on the slender statement that *Enoch walked with God: and he* was *not; for God took him,* the exegetes created a vast lore, giving in great detail Enoch's occupation (a shoemaker), his behavior in a world of wicked men, and an account of how he was treated when he was taken up to Heaven to serve near the Divine Throne. Of particular interest is the claim that when Enoch entered Heaven, his body turned into celestial fire and he was constantly surrounded by thunder and lightning, storms and whirlwinds. For this may have been the origin of the idea that the appearances of the shoemaker Ahasuerus were accompanied by thunderstorms and inclement weather.

2. Abraham's Prayer

A VARIATION of the belief that there are men so righteous that God grants them to "abide forever" is the belief that there are men so favored in the eyes of the Lord that they can pray for anything, and their prayers will be granted, and the Angel of Death has no power over them. But man's wish for longevity is tempered by resentment of the handicaps of old age; and this ambivalence toward longevity is part of the Legend of the Wandering Jew. Both attitudes are given in a legend, now many centuries old, about Abraham, found in the *Midrash Rabbah* and once current before the fifth century A.D.

The legend tells that Abraham, after Sarah's death, married a woman named Keturah and was *full with the strength of youth.* He looked forward to raising a large family and wished to live on forever.

Now, there was no one more favored in the eyes of the Lord than Abraham. And God listened to Abraham's prayer and then said to him: "Because you have walked before Me in truth and in faith, your soul will not be taken from you unless you pray for death. But the laws of nature shall not be changed for you, and it is the law that all men are mortal, and that all mortals must age."

Years passed. Abraham and his wife Keturah had many sons who in turn later multiplied and established such great tribes as the Midianites, the Ishbakites, and the Dedanites. And still Abraham wished to live on.

One day a very old man came to Abraham's door begging for food. Abraham took him in. The old man's knees trembled and he faltered as he walked, both because his muscles were weak and his eyes were dim. When Abraham served him food, the old man could not hold the spoon in his shaking hands and the food spilled over his garments. Abraham watched him with great pity and a troubled heart.

"How old are you?" Abraham asked his guest.

"Just a few years older than you," the old man replied. "But such are the laws of nature that when one reaches a certain age, the senses wither like flowers in autumn."

After the old man left, Abraham bowed his head and lifted up his voice in prayer: "O Lord! Let me die with the strength of my senses still undiminished and before I become a burden to myself and my kin." And God heard his prayer and sent the Angel of Death for Abraham's soul.

Many other legends in the rabbinic literature of that period point up this ambivalence of man toward longevity. In one legend there is a whole city—the City of Luz—over which the Angel of Death has no power. The dwellers of that city never die so long as they remain within its boundaries. But in time, according to the legend, people tire of living, and they find a way out of the city gates. And as soon as they reach the outer walls, they die.

3. Elijah the Prophet

THE most dramatic instance of a mortal who did not *taste of death* is to be found in the story of the Prophet Elijah who, when his time came to die, *went up by a whirlwind into heaven* (II Kings 2:11).

In post-Biblical folklore a great number of legends arose that reflected the belief that ever since Elijah's translation to heaven, he spends half his time on earth, wandering throughout the world to bring solace and hope. This vast number of legends about Elijah's wanderings preceded the legends of Cartaphilus-Ahasuerus-Laquedem by many centuries. But, in essence, they all convey the same message: there is a man in the world who, by the will of God, did not *taste of death*, and who appears as a constant reminder to mankind of the Coming of the Messiah.

The legends describe Elijah as sometimes visible and at other times invisible. But he always comes to protect the innocent, to help the widow and the orphan, and to make justice prevail. "Owing to his ubiquitousness and to the universal belief that he remained, after his departure from the earth, the ever-ready helper of the Jew," states the *Jewish Encyclopedia,* "Elijah the prophet became the prototype of the Wandering Jew."

Traditionally, Elijah is beloved and honored in many ways. In every synagogue there is a seat upon which no one dares to sit, as it is reserved for the Prophet Elijah; and it is known as "Elijah's seat." For Elijah is the godfather of every Jewish infant that is circumcised. And once every year, during the ceremonial feast on the first eve of the Passover, Elijah, according to tradition, visits every Jewish household. A silver cup, called "Elijah's cup," is filled with wine and placed on the celebrants' table; and at a fixed time in the ritual the door is opened and the prophet welcomed in with joyful song. Many of the devout believe that those who watch closely, though they are not permitted to see the prophet, may observe the surface of the wine in Elijah's cup quiver, as he partakes of their feast.

On other occasions on which he makes his appearance the people do not know his identity until after he has performed his good deed and wandered on. He may appear as a beggar, or a shoemaker, or a water carrier. Sometimes he comes as a court official or as a bailiff. Whatever the guise needed at the moment for him to perform his good deed, that guise he assumes.

In the entire range of Biblical folklore there is not another personage who has stimulated folk imagination more than Elijah. Myriads of wonders and miracles are attributed to him. All his deeds are also object-lessons, often suffused with humor.

In one story Elijah appeared as an old Arab beggar to a poor man who was working in a field.

"Is the work hard, my son?" asked the Arab.

"Our forefathers in Egypt worked harder, and they were better than I," the man answered.

"What makes you think they were better?"

"They were found worthy to live in the days of Moses and Aaron, and we live in the days when the spy and the thief accumulate riches but the honest man earns only starvation."

"Tell me," said the old beggar, "if you were offered seven years of wealth and plenty, would you want them now or at the end of your life?"

The man replied: "You must be a wizard, and I shall have nothing to do with you. Go in peace!"

But the old Arab persisted and repeated his question three times. Finally the man said: "I am married. Whatever I choose my wife will have to share in. She should therefore also share in my decision and choice."

That evening, after the children had gone to bed, the man told his wife about the incident with the Arab, and asked her which she would choose, if given the choice.

"I would want the seven good years right now," she answered. "For if they came at the end of our lives, we would know the end was near, and that would embitter every happy day for us."

The husband agreed. And when the beggar again appeared in the field, asking the same question, the man told him he would take the good years immediately. And the old Arab disappeared.

When the man returned from the field that evening, his wife came running toward him, full of the joyful news that their children had found a great treasure of gold beneath the ashes in their courtyard.

The next seven years were prosperous ones, and the man and his wife devoted themselves in them to helping the widow and the orphan, to sending children of the poor to school, to visiting the sick, and to comforting the bereaved.

At the end of seven years the man met the old Arab in the marketplace.

"The seven years have come to an end," the old Arab said, "and I have come for the treasure which the Lord lent to you."

"I consulted my wife before I accepted your offer," said the man. "May I consult her now that you have called for the return of the wealth?"

"Go and ask her, my son, and bring me her answer tomorrow at this very hour and in this place."

That evening the man said to his wife, "Suppose the treasure our children found was really lent to us for seven years and suppose the lender called for it now, what would you say?"

"I would say to him that if he can find people who will do more good with it, they are welcome to it."

The next day the man met the old Arab in the market-place and gave him the wife's answer.

"I will go in search of them without delay," said the old man, "and as soon as I find them, I will return for the money."

The old Arab disappeared, and the good man never saw him again.

Books have been filled with similar stories about Elijah, who wanders over the world to teach men to be good. Yet these deeds are trifling in comparison with what is expected of him in the days to come. For Elijah, it is believed, has been chosen to herald the coming of the Messiah. And three days before the Advent of the Messiah, Elijah will appear to prepare the people. On the third day the Messiah will appear with Elijah beside him. And then all the prophecies of the Messianic Age will be fulfilled.

Elijah is also prominent in Moslem lore. He is often called "Al-Khedr [The Green]" because he is credited with the discovery of the River of Youth. And the Wandering Jew in Moslem lore is often also called "Zerib bar Elia [The Prophet Elijah]", as he is named in *Fadilah and the Stranger.*

Curiously enough, the Christian belief that the Antichrist will appear to herald the Second Coming resembles in many respects the belief in the saintly Elijah as the herald of the Messiah, and may have been based on it. For in folklore we often find represented as profane what, in another time and belief, was sacred, or as depraved what elsewhere was noble.

The transformation of Elijah, the Judaic version of the Wandering Jew and the herald of the Messiah, into Ahasuerus, the Christian version of the same personage, and the Antichrist, heralding the Second Coming, exemplifies how folklore may transform a saintly character into an ignoble one.

4. The Thirty-six Wanderers

ACCORDING to an ancient rabbinic legend, there are, in fact, not one but thirty-six Wandering Jews, whose mission it is to help the deserving, to console and protect the widow, the orphan, and the aged, and ailing, and, above all, to remind people that if they have implicit faith all will be well with them and the world.

The existence of these Wanderers is explained in this way:

When the wickedness of man, in the days of Noah, became so great that *it repented the Lord that he had made man on the earth* (Genesis 6:6), and He decided to destroy all living things in a great flood, He remembered the righteous and whole-hearted Noah. And He spared Noah and his offspring in an ark made of gopher wood.

Later, when the flood subsided, God made a covenant with Noah and his children never again to destroy all living creatures. But knowing that mankind would again and again fill the earth with corruption and wickedness, and that He would be grieved and wish to destroy all mankind for its evildoing, He created seventy-two saints; thirty-six He placed in Heaven to be always beside Him to plead for their erring brothers on earth, and thirty-six he scattered over the earth. (In some versions of this legend thirty-six of the saints are in Jerusalem and the others in the rest of the world.) And when man's wickedness on earth multiplies and the Lord again regrets that He created man and wishes to destroy him, He remembers the thirty-six righteous ones on earth, and for their sake He spares all mankind.

The Thirty-Six are known as the "Lamed-Vaw Tzadikim [The Thirty-Six Righteous]." (In Hebrew the letters of the alphabet are used as numerals, and the letters *l (lamed)* and *v (vaw)* represent *30* and *6;* the two letters together also mean *him.* And reading the passage: *Happy are they who wait for* him (Isiah 30:18), the rabbis concluded that the number of saintly ones who wait must be thirty-six—hence, the Lamed-Vaw Tzadikim.)

The Thirty-Six never appear jointly. They, like the Three Nephites, invariably appear singly. Nor does anyone know him as one of the Thirty-Six until after he has performed his good deed and disappeared. That is why each of them is also called a "Nistar The Mysterious One]."

The Mysterious One appears as the lowliest of the lowly; by profession a shoemaker or a cordwainer or a tailor, outwardly never learned and often illiterate, he is always abstemious, and goes about his work with great humility. By his humility and goodness one may suspect, though never be certain, of being in the presence of a Nistar. (And that is why, the rabbis go on to say, one must treat with reverence anyone who is good and humble, particularly if he is poor and uneducated. For he might be one of the Thirty-Six for whose sake the world is preserved.)

The good deeds of the Thirty-Six are beyond count, as might be expected, in their ministering to a people in exile for centuries, and whose troubles were many. Often the legends about the Thirty-Six have become confused (or interwoven) with Elijah the Prophet, the prototype of the Wandering Jew; and the Thirty-Six were probably prototypes of the Three Nephites of The Book of Mormon. By their professions and activities, their poverty and humility, they may have contributed to the legend of Ahasuerus the shoemaker who awaits the Judgment Day.

5. The Sleepers

A VARIATION of the Legend of the Wandering Jew is to be found in the numerous myths about the man whose life was prolonged miraculously in sleep, and through whom is demonstrated the conviction that those who pray for the blessing of an abnormally long life pray to their own hurt.

HONI THE CIRCLE-MAKER

One of the most memorable of these "sleepers" (it is claimed that he might have been a member of the Thirty-Six) was Honi the Circle-Maker.

Honi (according to the Palestinian Talmud) was a great Essene teacher, a direct descendant of Moses, who lived in the first century B.C. His goodness and piety were such that whatever he prayed for was fulfilled. And this is how he prayed: He would draw a circle on the ground, then step into its center. Within the circle he prayed and prayed, vowing not to leave its boundaries until his prayers were granted. He never prayed for himself, nor did he ever pray for anything outside the bounds of God's mercy. He prayed for rain; he prayed for health; he prayed for peace. But he never prayed that a curse befall anyone, not even on the cruellest enemy. Because his prayers were always granted, he gained the reputation of a miracle worker. And he was nicknamed "the Circle-Maker."

Honi was walking on the outskirts of his town one day, absorbed in thought, reflecting on the meaning of the passage: *For thus saith the Lord, That after seventy years be accomplished at Babylon, I will visit you, and perform my good word toward you, in causing you to return to this place* (Jeremiah 29:10). Could men sleep for seventy years, Honi wondered? And what would it be like to waken almost a century after going to sleep? Honi was tempted to pray that he should be allowed to sleep seventy years and then awaken so that he might look upon the world of that time.

As he looked up, he saw a very old man in an orchard planting a carob tree. Honi greeted him and drew nearer.

"Tell me," he asked, "how long does it take for a carob tree to grow and bear fruit?"

"Seventy years," replied the graybeard.

"And do you expect to live to eat of its fruit?"

"No. But when I was born there were already fruit-bearing carob trees which were planted by my forefathers. As they planted those trees for me, I plant for my grandchildren."

Honi sat down on the ground with his back against a tree and began to chew on a carob pod, as he talked to the old man. In a little while Honi became drowsy and fell asleep.

When he awoke he found himself completely covered by a layer of twigs and dry leaves. Honi made his way out of the heap, and there he saw before him a man gathering the fruit of the carob. .

"Are you the man who planted this tree?" Honi asked.

"No," the man replied. "It was planted by my grandfather."

Honi was puzzled by the reply and kept thinking about it as he returned to town. But he found the town greatly changed, and he knew none of the people he met there. He asked a stranger: "Do you know the son of Honi the Circle-Maker?" And the man replied: "He is long since dead. But his grandson still lives." And he directed Honi to the place where Honi might find his grandson. But when Honi arrived there and said that he was Honi the Circle-Maker, his grandson and family scoffed at him and would not believe him.

Then Honi went outside and drew a circle on the ground. He stepped into the middle of the circle and prayed for death, for his loneliness was greater than he could bear. And so he died.

Since legends never appear singly, there are variations in the story on how long Honi slept, and the way he died.

THE SEVEN SLEEPERS
OF EPHESUS

Legends of "sleepers" were known before Honi's days, and many arose after his time. There is John the Divine who sleeps in his grave, the ground heaving over his breast as he breathes; and he waits to awaken and appear as a witness against the Antichrist before the Second Coming; there is Joseph of Arimathea, who helped take Jesus down from the Cross, and who lies in the city of Sarras, drawing perpetual life from the Holy Grail. Charlemagne, it is believed, sleeps in the heart of a mountain, fully armed and crowned, waiting for the hour when he will awaken and come out to release the Franks from oppression. And there is Merlin, the magician in King Arthur's court, who was spellbound by the wicked Vivien and imprisoned in an old oak tree in the forest of Broceliande, where he sleeps fitfully to this day. And so on.

The most celebrated of the legends about "sleepers" is the story of The Seven Sleepers of Ephesus, which has appeared with subtle variations in many Oriental languages, and the episode has been commemorated in hymns and liturgical texts.

The Seven Sleepers were seven Christians of Ephesus who lived in the days of Emperor Gaius Messius Quintus Decius, the cruel ruler who so bitterly persecuted Christians. These seven Christians (whose names were

Maximimian, Malchus, Martinian, Dionysius, John, Serapion and Constantine) came before the Emperor and openly proclaimed themselves as Christians who refused to sacrifice to the Roman idols. Emperor Decius gave them three days in which to change their minds or face execution for heresy.

The Seven took advantage of this time to dispose of their worldly goods among the poor; and then they fled, all seven of them, to a cave in Mount Celion. And there the Seven fell asleep.

When they failed to present themselves before Decius at the appointed time, the Emperor sent men out to search for them; and he ordered the mouths of all caves blocked with stones, so that if they had sought refuge in a cavern they would perish of hunger.

Three hundred and sixty years passed. By that time Emperor Theodosius was building a stable and his workers went to Mount Celion for stones. Finding the stones they sought near a cave, they took them away, and the mouth of the cave was opened. Instantly the Seven Sleepers awoke, but they thought they had slept but one night. And they said to Malchus, who was their spokesman: "Go to the city and buy some bread for us. And find out what Decius plans to do."

Malchus took some coins and went to the city. But as he reached Ephesus he stopped to look with incredulity at the cross over the city gate. He walked around to another city gate, and there he saw another cross. He walked on, and the sign of the cross was on every gate. Finally Malchus entered the city. But everything seemed strange to him. And stranger still was the talk of the people, for often they repeated the Lord's name, which only yesterday, Malchus thought, had been forbidden. Malchus concluded that he might have entered the wrong city. He stopped a stranger and asked for the name of the city, and the stranger looked at him in surprise, and answered: "Ephesus!"

Then Malchus remembered his hungry friends in the

cave, and he hastened to a baker's shop and asked for bread, putting his coins down in payment. The baker examined the coins in astonishment and showed them to several other customers who were present; then he asked Malchus where he had found the treasure. When Malchus protested that he had no knowledge of any treasure, the baker and the others in the shop bound him with a rope and dragged him to the marketplace. A great crowd quickly gathered, and the rumor began to travel that a youth had discovered a great treasure and refused to divulge the place where he had found it. When the news reached the governor, he ordered Malchus brought before him for interrogation.

"What is your name?" he was asked.

"Malchus."

"Where are you from?"

"I am a native of Ephesus, if this be Ephesus."

"Do your parents live here?"

Malchus assured the governor that they did, and gave the names of his parents and of all his relatives. But no such people were known to anyone in Ephesus.

"Where did you get these coins?" they wanted to know.

"They are mine."

"How can they be yours when they date back three hundred and seventy-seven years?" he was asked.

"I implore you," Malchus pleaded, "in the name of God, permit me to ask you some questions."

His request was granted. And at once Malchus asked what had happened to Emperor Decius.

"Emperor Decius died centuries ago," he was answered.

Then Malchus told the governor that he and his six companions had been persecuted by Decius because they were Christians, they had sought refuge in a cave in Mount Celion, and there they had slept, he thought, one night. Malchus then led the governor to the cave, with a great crowd following them. And when the governor saw the martyrs in the cave, their faces fresh as roses, he fell upon his knees and praised the Lord. Word was sent to Theodosius, and the Emperor came to do honor to the Seven Sleepers of Ephesus.

Many versions of this legend are known the world over. The legends of the "sleepers" have stimulated the imagination of many writers, who began to use this theme. Washington Irving's *Rip Van Winkle* is a notable example. Earlier, the legends of the "sleepers" resulted in a variety of romantic folk tales, which found favor with children of all ages, one of which, the story of *The Sleeping Beauty,* is a special favorite.

In the story *The Sleeping Beauty* a lovely young princess, because of the curse of an angry fairy, falls asleep for a hundred years. But at the same moment the young princess falls into the enchanted sleep, her father and mother and all the people in the court also fall asleep. Not only the king and queen and all their courtiers and palace guards and servants slept, but even the horses in the stables, the pigeons in the lofts, the dogs beneath the tables, and the flies upon the walls—all fell asleep for exactly one hundred years. At the end of a hundred years a prince discovers the sleeping beauty, falls in love with her, and kisses her. Instantly she awakens, and at the same moment everyone else in the palace awakens. The guards begin to present arms; the cooks begin to season the food; the dogs begin to bark; and even the flies on the walls begin to buzz. They all live happily to the end of their days—in another century.

But the curse of the angry fairy would have been an unbearable doom if the princess had awakened a century later to find all her people dead and forgotten. For that is the bitter part of the doom of the Wandering Jew. He must remain changeless, or return to his young manhood every seventy years, whereas all the people he has come to know grow old and infirm, and die.

The numerous legends about "sleepers" reflect man's concern with the brevity of life and his speculations on what it would be like to sleep for a century, or centuries, and then awaken to see the world of that time. It is obviously a recurrent theme in the Legend of the Wandering Jew.

6. The Influence of the Jatakas

THERE are some scholars who maintain that the Legend of the Wandering Jew really had its inception in the Hindu concept of reincarnation, and was influenced by the Buddhist birth fables, the Jatakas. Reincarnation is the belief that the soul is deathless and that it transmigrates from one body, which in death decays, to another, newly born. In the Hindu belief reincarnation comes under the karmic law, which stipulates that from good must come good and from evil, evil. The transmigrated soul is therefore affected in successive lives by the kind of existence it led in a preceding life. The good done in one life is rewarded in a succeeding life, the evil in one punished in another.

Buddhism stresses the essential oneness of the universe and the doctrine that the individual soul is not a separate entity but a part, a particle, a mere proton, of the world soul—with which each soul strives to unite. The soul can reach its ultimate goal and unite with the world soul only after reaching perfection, or Enlightenment, through successive lives of saintliness and wisdom. And when a soul reaches the ultimate state of Enlightenment, it enters nirvana, which is the state of union with the world soul, and it is no longer subject to reincarnation.

The Buddhist scriptures present five hundred and fifty incidents or fables, called Jatakas, which narrate the incarnations of Gautama the Buddha demonstrating his wisdom and goodness, and his life as a bodhisattva, before he attained Enlightenment and became the Buddha. And the implication is clear that any soul that chooses saintliness and the good life can ultimately become a Buddha. For Buddhahood, open to all who are willing to strive for it, is the road to nirvana—just as the life in Christ, for Christians, is the road to the Kingdom of Heaven.

The basic recurrent idea in the Legend of the Wandering Jew is that the Wanderer seeks redemption so that he might be worthy of entering the Heavenly Kingdom. Instead of dying and being reincarnated in successive generations, he goes to sleep every seventy years and awakens as a young man of thirty, and starts again on the road of penance, seeking redemption, until he becomes Christlike—which is the Christian equivalent of Buddhahood.

Even in the West the will to believe in reincarnation and the remembrance of past lives is shown in the eager support given stories in which people, under hypnosis or in a state of trance, can recall events of past lives with great clarity and accuracy. These instances are used to attempt to establish, presumably upon an unshakable foundation, the acceptance and belief of metempsychosis.

Many books have been written on the topics of karma and reincarnation by Theosophists, Rosicrucians, parapsychologists, metaphysicians, and mystics—and the great success of their books is proof of the eagerness with which a large number of people are ready to accept the doctrine of reincarnation.

Some twentieth-century writers, who have used the Wandering Jew as symbol, have presented the Wanderer not as existing bodily for a number of centuries, but as the inheritor, generation after generation, of a shattering human weakness which, at the time of crisis, he remembers as having belonged to his father and his grandfather before him, and so on for many preceding generations.

7. Mortality in Primitive Folklore

CONCERN with longevity, death, and immortality began, as far as can be discerned, with primitive man—whose reflections we can dimly perceive in lingering customs and beliefs. And these subjects were of interest not only to the religious leaders of those early times but to all the people, since to everyone living comes, soon or late, the *taste of death*.

The questions which have been asked since the earliest times are: Is death natural and inevitable? Is death final, or is there a life hereafter? Could life be indefinitely extended, and would that be desirable?

Most primitive peoples believed that man was naturally immortal, and that mortality was caused by visible enemies, by disease, and by invisible witchcraft. The prime cause of death was witchcraft; and sorcery was considered the most effective method of combating death, as magic was the accepted way of banishing disease, and thus preventing unnatural death. As a protection against witchcraft and disease various amulets and charms were prescribed which had the magic power of preventing these evils from attacking the wearers. Amulets are still worn by men and women of different religions the world over as protection from evil and disease. Some charms are used to protect dwellings and to frustrate the spells of witchcraft and evil spirits. There are places even today where people place horseshoes under their doorsteps to keep illness and misfortune from entering their homes.

But if a talisman failed, and a man died an "unnatural" death, what happened to his soul? (That man has a soul was accepted by all primitive peoples, though concepts of the soul differed greatly.) Primitive peoples often believed that the soul was indestructible and deathless, and that there was a life hereafter for all souls which depart from their bodies. From primitive worship of the dead we infer that primitive peoples considered the dead to have conscious personalities and to remain interested and influential in the affairs of the world of the living. For this reason, the souls of the dead were propitiated to induce their favor, and they were appealed to in time of need for help.

The place where departed souls congregate was a mystery the priests tried to solve, and they arrived at different conclusions. Almost all agreed that the just and the unjust, good men and evil men, do not go to the same hereafter: the good go to "heaven"; and the bad go to "hell". These places were conceived and described differently, depending upon the temperaments of the originators, who gave us the Elysian Fields, the Islands of the Blessed, Paradise, Valhalla, the Happy Hunting Grounds, and the Mohammedan *Falay al Aflak*—for the righteous, and Hades, the pit of Acheron, Gehenna, and so on—for the wicked.

With the rise of the belief that all departed souls either must go to one of the abodes of heaven for an everlasting and blissful existence, or go into one of the lakes of fire and brimstone for interminable torture, the fear of death intensified. And to ameliorate this fear, hope was given to those who had not yet earned the right to celestial bliss, of mending their ways in successive rebirths.

But no matter how convinced people were about the

life hereafter and reincarnation, the cynics and pessimists among them constantly reminded them that life is fleeting and the end uncertain.

The brevity of life and the certainty of death was summed up by the Persian poet, Omar Khayyam, of the twelfth century:

> Oh threats of Hell and Hopes of Paradise!
> One thing at least is certain—This life flies;
> One thing is certain and the rest is Lies;
> The flower that once had blown for ever dies.

And he adds:

> Strange, is it not? that of the myriads who
> Before us pass'd the door of Darkness through,
> Not one returns to tell us of the Road,
> Which to discover we must travel too.

The strength of death over all is given in the Talmud: "A mountain is strong, but iron can destroy it; iron is strong, but fire can melt it; fire is strong, but water can extinguish it; water is strong, but it can be evaporated into clouds; clouds are strong, but the wind can scatter them; wind is strong, but man can conquer it; the body is strong, but fear can break it; fear is strong, but wine can drive it out; wine is strong, but sleep can diminish it; but death is stronger than all of them."

Nevertheless man hoped to prolong the period between birth and death. In every generation there were people who dreamed of discovering a magic formula or medicine that would double or triple man's normal span of life. Yet even these dreamers often awoke with misgivings. For as they reflected on longevity with detachment, grievous doubts arose in their minds that prolonging life indefinitely would be a blessing. From the time of Abraham's prayer for death, and of the venerable dwellers of the City of Luz who could endure living no longer, to the present day, the doubt about the desirability of longevity repeatedly arises.

In a work compiled nearly eighteen centuries ago, *The Ethics of the Fathers* (*Pirke Abot*), fourteen stages in a man's life are described, and the last five given are: "At sixty a man attains old age; at seventy the hoary head; at eighty the gift of special strength; at ninety he bends beneath the weight of his years; at a hundred he is as if he were already dead and had passed away from the world." Obviously, it profits no one to live that long.

Physicians specializing in geriatrics sadly conclude that the prolonging of life, without first banishing the ailments and deterioration that accompany old age, is not a boon but a curse. And they, like some ancients, feel that we ought to devote ourselves to the discovery of the Fountain of Youth rather than the River of Longevity.

As can be readily seen, the "curse of longevity," which is a basic theme in the Legend of the Wandering Jew, has very deep roots. Theodor Reik, the noted psychologist, in his book *Myth and Guilt* writes: "It is not unlikely that the great poet who wrote the Book of Job took his material from an old folk tale as Aeschylus borrowed his plot from an ancient myth. . . . There are late offshoots, for instance the Legend of the Wandering Jew, of that figure of the deathless old man who roams the earth, cursed with immortality. . . . It is obvious that the Wandering Jew personified the old Father-God, but the figure should also explain the fate of His worshippers who had to wander from one country to another. In late literary usages of the legend . . . the Eternal Jew appears sometimes as Jahveh, sometimes as Jesus Himself."

8. Swift's Immortals

ONE of the most devastating commentaries on longevity is to be found in Jonathan Swift's *Gulliver's Travels*. On his third voyage—following his adventures in Lilliput and Brobdingnag—Gulliver visits several countries in the Eastern seas, Luggnagg among them. While enjoying the hospitality of the King of Luggnagg and the courtesy of the proud Luggnaggians, Gulliver tries to acquire a knowledge of the ways and customs of that strange land.

"One day in much good company, I was asked by a person of quality, whether I had seen any of their *Struldbrugs* or *Immortals*. I said I had not; and desired he would explain to me what he meant by such an appellation applied to a mortal creature. He told me, that sometimes, though very rarely, a child happened to be born in a family with a red circular spot in the forehead, directly over the left eyebrow, which was an infallible mark that it should never die. . . . That these productions were not peculiar to any family, but a mere effect of chance; and the children of the *struldbrugs* themselves were equally mortal with the rest of the people.

On hearing this, Gulliver cries out in rapture: "Happy nation, where every child hath at least a chance for being immortal! Happy people who enjoy so many living examples of ancient virtue, and have masters ready to instruct them in the wisdom of all former ages: but, happiest beyond all comparison are those excellent *struldbrugs*, who being born exempt from that universal calamity of human nature, have their minds free and disengaged, without the weight and depression of spirits caused by the continual apprehension of death."

After discussing the matter among themselves in their own language, not one word of which Gulliver understood, his hosts ask him politely how he vizualizes the life he would have led if he had been born an immortal.

"I answered, it was easy to be eloquent on so copious and delightful a subject . . . And upon this very case I had frequently run over the whole system how I should employ myself and pass the time if I were sure to live for ever.

"That if it had been my good fortune to come into the world a *struldbrug,* as soon as I could discover my own happiness by understanding the difference between life and death, I would first resolve by all arts and methods whatsoever to procure myself riches. In the pursuit of which, by thrift and management, I might reasonably expect, in about two hundred years, to be the wealthiest man in the kingdom. In the second place, I would from my earliest youth apply myself to the study of arts and sciences, by which I should arrive in time to excel all others in learning. Lastly, I would carefully record every action and event of consequence that happened in the public, impartially draw the characters of the several successions of princes and great ministers of state, with my own observations on every point. I would exactly set down the several changes in customs, language, fashions of dress, diet and diversions. By all which acquirements, I should be a living treasury of knowledge and wisdom, and certainly become the oracle of the nation.

"I would never marry after threescore, but live in an hospitable manner, yet still on the saving side. I would entertain myself in forming and directing the minds of hopeful young men, by convincing them from my own remembrance, experience and observation, fortified by numerous examples, of the usefulness of virtue in public and private life. But my choice and constant companions should be a set of my own immortal brotherhood, among whom I would elect a dozen from the most ancient down to my own contemporaries. Where any of these wanted fortunes, I would provide them with convenient lodges round my own estate, and have some of them always at my table, only mingling a few of the most valuable among you mortals, whom length of time would harden me to lose with little or no reluctance, and treat your posterity after the same manner; just as a man diverts himself with the annual succession of pinks and tulips in his garden, without regretting the loss of those which withered the preceding year.

"These *struldbrugs* and I would mutually communicate our observations and memorials through the course of time, remark the several gradations by which corruption steals into the world, and oppose it in every step, by giving perpetual warning and instruction to mankind; which, added to the strong influence of our own example, would probably prevent that continual degeneracy of human nature, so justly complained of in all ages.

"Add to all this the pleasure of seeing the various revolutions of states and empires, the changes in the lower and upper world, ancient cities in ruins, and obscure villages become the seats of kings. Famous rivers lessening into shallow brooks, the ocean leaving one coast dry, and overwhelming another; the discovery of many countries yet unknown. Barbarity overrunning the politest nations, and the most barbarous become civilized. I should then see the discovery of the longitude, the perpetual motion, the universal medicine, and many other great inventions brought to the utmost perfection.

"What wonderful discoveries should we make in astronomy, by outliving and confirming our own predictions, by observing the progress and returns of comets, with the changes of motion in the sun, moon and stars."

After Gulliver finishes his enthusiastic response, his hosts begin to talk excitedly among themselves, punctuating their lively conversation with bursts of laughter. Finally they tell Gulliver they have observed that people in countries other than their own avidly desire longevity, and that "whoever had one foot in the grave, was sure to hold back the other as strongly as he could" and "the oldest had still hopes of living one day longer." But this is not the case in Luggnagg, because the Luggnaggians have the continual example of the Immortals before them.

Then Gulliver is given an account of the life of these Immortals in Luggnagg, who, up to the age of thirty, live and act like ordinary and normal people, "after which by degrees they grew melancholy and dejected, increasing in both till they came to fourscore. . . . When they came to fourscore years, which is reckoned the extremity of living in this country, they had not only all the follies and infirmities of other old men, but many more which arose from the dreadful prospect of never dying. They were not only opinionative, peevish, covetous, morose, vain, talkative, but uncapable of friendship, and dead to all natural affection, which never descended below their grandchildren. Envy and impotent desires are their prevailing passions. But those objects against which their envy seems principally directed, are the vices of the younger sort, and the deaths of the old. By reflecting on the former, they find themselves cut off from all possibility of pleasure; and whenever they see a funeral, they lament and repine that others have gone to an harbour of rest, to which they themselves never can hope to arrive. They have no remembrance of anything but what they learned and observed in their youth and middle age, and even that is very imperfect. And for the truth or particulars of any fact, it is safer to depend on common traditions than upon their best recollections. The least miserable among them, appear to be those who turn to dotage, and entirely lose their memories; these meet with more pity and assistance, because they want many bad qualities which abound in others. . . .

"As soon as they have completed the term of eighty years, they are looked on as dead in law; their heirs immediately succeed to their estates, only a small pittance is reserved for their support, and the poor ones are maintained at the public charge. After that period they are held incapable of any employment of trust or profit; they cannot purchase lands or take leases, neither are they allowed to be witnesses in any cause, either civil or criminal, not even for the decision of meers and bounds.

"At ninety they lose their teeth and hair, they have at that age no distinction of taste, but eat and drink whatever they can get, without relish or appetite. The diseases they were subject to still continue without increasing or diminishing. In talking they forget the common appellation of things, and the names of persons, even of those who are their nearest friends and relations. For the same reason they never can amuse themselves with reading, because their memory will not serve to carry them from the beginning of a sentence to the end; and by this defect they are deprived of the only entertainment whereof they might otherwise be capable.

"The language of this country being always upon the flux, the *struldbrugs* of one age do not understand those of another; neither are they able after two hundred years to hold any conversation (farther than by a few general words) with their neighbours the mortals; and thus they lie under the disadvantage of living like foreigners in their own country."

After this discussion, Gulliver has the opportunity to observe several of the Immortals, and what he has been told is confirmed.

Gulliver then remarks that "from what I had heard and seen, my keen appetite for perpetuity of life was much abated . . . and thought no tyrant could invent a death into which I would not run with pleasure from such a life."

Gulliver's conclusion was the same as had been expressed in many versions of the Legend of the Wandering Jew. In them we find the Wanderer often longs to die, and there is no death to which he would not run with pleasure to terminate his weary life.

9. From Koheleth to Kafka

W E thus find that the roots of the Legend of the Wandering Jew, like the roots of all universal legends, go down deep into the dark recesses of a perplexing question and draw sustenance from diverse elements in the attempt to give the answer, if not as an acceptable solution, then at least as a unified presentation. Close to the surface, the roots of the legend seem to sprout from the Biblical passages we have quoted. But the deeper we probe the clearer it becomes that the legend has its origin in an age-old riddle that has troubled man's mind ever since he was capable of reflecting upon it and which puzzles him to this day.

The two basic themes in the Legend of the Wandering Jew are presented with infinite variation: one is the curse of abnormal longevity, and the conviction that for him who is so cursed *it had been good for that man if he had not been born*; and the other is the problem of guilt and absolution—the road of penance a man must travel to reach redemption. The first theme is the essence of pessimism; the second, the very heart of optimism. For one declares the utter vanity of existence, and the other proclaims there is a way that gives meaning to human existence and allows men to die undefeated.

The literature of the world echoes and re-echoes the anguished cry about the vanity of living and the longing to cease from troubling and to be at rest in death.

In the *Book of Job* there is the bitter outcry: *Why died I not from the womb?* And Job reflects how good it would have been had he died at birth.

> *For now should I have lain still and been quiet,*
> *I should have slept: then had I been at rest,*
> *With kings and counselors of the earth,*
> *Which built desolate places for themselves;*
> *Or with princes that had gold,*
> *Who filled their houses with silver: . . .*
> *The small and great are there;*
> *And the servant is free from his master.*

(Job 3:13-20).

And throughout the debate with his sanctimonious friends—who argue that Job is afflicted because he must have sinned and the punishment fits his transgression— Job comes back again and again to his lament, *My soul is weary of my life*: And he pleads with God:

> Are *not my days few? cease* then,
> *And let me alone, that I may take comfort a little,*
> *Before I go* whence *I shall not return,*
> Even *to the land of darkness and the shadow of death;*
> *A land of darkness, as darkness* itself;
> And *of the shadow of death, without any order,*
> *And* where *the light* is *as darkness.*

(Job 10:20-24)

Though less bitter, yet even more profoundly pessimistic, is Koheleth the author of Ecclesiastes, who conceives of man's years, at best, as a concatenation of vain and meaningless days repeating, with only slight variation, absurdity after absurdity.

Vanity of vanities, saith the Preacher; all is *vanity:*

And Koheleth expresses his contempt for an existence in which there are no values: . . . *As it happeneth to the fool, so it happeneth even to me; and why was I then more wise? Then I said in my heart, that this also is vanity. For there is no remembrance of the wise more than of the fool for ever; seeing that which is now in the days to come shall all be forgotten. And how dieth the wise* man? *as the fool* (Ecclesiastes 2:15-16).

And when Koheleth enumerates all the things for which there is a season, the first is *a time to be born, and a time to die.* He is a blessed man who dies in his season; and cursed is he who lingers on until he is *as if he were already dead.* Koheleth comes back to this thought repeatedly: *And the day of death* [is better] *than the day of one's birth.* Not only is life absurd and full of pain, but the will whereby life operates is also incredibly unjust. *I returned, and saw under the sun, that the race* is *not to the swift, nor the battle to the strong, neither yet bread to the wise, nor yet riches to men of understanding, nor yet favor to men of skill; but time and chance happeneth to them all* (Ecclesiastes 9:11).

These doubts were not peculiar to Job and Koheleth. They are reflected in such disparate works, in widely separated generations, as the Sumero-Babylonian *Dialogue in Pessimism* and the writings of Franz Kafka. Over and over again we hear the cry that not to be born would be best for mortal men, and, once born, not to outlive one's generation is the second-best blessing man can wish for.

A Jobian pessimism is also reflected by Sigmund Freud, who gives in his *Wit and Its Relation to the Unconscious,* this example of nonsense wit: "Never to be born would be best for mortal men, but this happens only to a very few."

In Ecclesiastes we find this crushing pessimism expressed in three words: *All is vanity:* In Buddhism, in which, according to some, the Legend of the Wandering

Jew has its roots, a vast religious system is devoted to what in Western terms is an acceptance of pessimism and "non-being." For Buddhism teaches that the ultimate goal of every man should be to reach nirvana, which is the release from reincarnation. It is the happy state in which the individual soul unites with the world-soul and is granted the Jobian-Freudian wish for the blessing of "not to be born" again.

Pessimism as a religious philosophy existed even before Buddhism in the Sumero-Babylonian belief that God equated with Fate, and that Fate was capricious and certainly unjust.

In modern times, the leading philosophies of pessimism were argued brilliantly by Arthur Schopenhauer and his disciple Karl Hartmann. They saw life as a complex of painful strivings and unappeased desires in a purposeless, pointless, irrational world of chance.

This pessimism, with the Wandering Jew symbolizing Everyman in search of forgetfulness in death, is expressed in many forms in literature. Even such a basically optimistic individual as Jean Cocteau, finds, as he tells us, that "living upsets me more than dying." In his *Moral Essays* he writes:

"On the subject of death, I have more to say. I am surprised that so many people are affected by it since it is in us each second and they should accept it with peace of mind. Why be afraid of a person with whom you live, closely joined with your own substance? We have become accustomed to making death into a legend and judging her from the outside. It would be better to say that at birth we marry her and adjust to her character, despite her roguishness. She is able to have herself forgotten and let us believe that she is no longer living in the house. Each one of us gives lodging to his death and is reassured by what he invents about her, namely that she is an allegorical figure appearing only in the last act."

Here we have a submission to death and an unspoken

gladness that she is always there from the start and that "The shorter my life becomes, the longer her life grows."

Franz Kafka, on the other hand, sees that "the first sign of the beginning of understanding is the wish to die." In his book *Dearest Father,* he tells us:

"This life appears unbearable; another unattainable. One is no longer ashamed of wanting to die; one asks to be moved from the old cell, which one hates, to a new one, which one will only in time come to hate. In this there is also a residue of belief that during the move the master will chance to come along the corridor, look at the prisoner, and say: 'This man is not to be locked up again. He is to come to me.'"

And in his mystic way, Kafka holds out the Buddhist hope of not being moved "from the old cell, which one hates, to a new one, which one will only in time come to hate" but of being freed forever in non-being.

Literature is replete with expressions that not only should one not be "ashamed of wanting to die" but that when the normal span of man is done, he should not seek to live another day.

It is therefore not at all surprising that in the figure of the Wandering Jew, both optimists concerned with redemption, and pessimists in search of "non-being," should have found a convenient armature upon which to mold their expressions and build their poems, novels, and dramas.

Part Three

THE LEGEND IN LITERATURE AND ART

"It is not unlikely that the great poet who wrote the Book of Job took his material from an old folk tale as Aeschylus borrowed his plot from an ancient myth. Myths were formed from the rich store of oral tradition and finally shaped into folk epics or plays as were those of Homer and of the Greek dramatists."

—THEODORE REIK IN *Myth and Guilt*

1. The Legend in Poetry

THE legends of the Wanderer, used as a theme to explore guilt-and-repentance-and-redemption in spectroscopic variations, and permeated with the "death wish," fascinated poets of the Western nations, particularly poets of the nineteenth century. Before that time the story of the Wanderer had been the subject of popular ballads, long narrative poems, and epic dramas; and the symbolic figure was accented in every meter in numerous brief poems to express crushing despair, unbearable doubt, or ecstatic penitence. The Wanderer became a favorite poetic symbol of the grief and tears of humanity, or was introduced by the poet as a witness of the spirit of an ancient revolt against fate, dating all the way back to the Sumero-Babylonian discourses on pessimism.

One of the first rhymed narratives extant, on the appearance of the Wandering Jew as described by the Armenian Archbishop at St. Albans was chronicled in Latin in 1243 by Philippe de Mousket, Bishop of Tournai. And from that day on there were, apparently, a number of narrative poems, such as the *Ballad of Brabant,* which were popular in their day.

Brief or lengthy treatments in poetry of the Legend of the Wandering Jew appeared in the Low countries and in the Slavic countries, in France and in Italy, and, later on, in England. But the Germans, more than any other peoples, were fascinated by the legend and its implications, and they have created the greatest body of poetry on the topic. From the end of the eighteenth century to the beginning of the twentieth century, almost every major and minor poet in Germany, directly or indirectly, coped with the symbol of the Wandering Jew.

The poet Christian Friedrich Daniel Schubart (1739-1791) long dwelled on the possibilities of the legend as a vehicle for his ideas about life's more unbearable burden—boredom. In his poem *Rhapsody,* he presents Ahasuerus as the man cursed not by Jesus but by the Angel of Death. His Ahasuerus sees Jerusalem fall, Rome destroyed, great nations disintegrate and perish, but he lives on through thousands of years. Ahasuerus experiences every conceivable pain and agony, but the sufferings of boredom are the greatest of them all. When he finally dies, an angel buries him with the consolation: "Sleep, Ahasuerus, sleep soundly: God's anger does not last forever!"

Early in the nineteenth century a number of German poets—Aloys Schreiber, Wilhelm Müller, Adelbert von Chamisso, August Wilhelm von Schlegel, and others—grappled with the legend in their poetry. But the most masterful treatment of the legend would have been the long epic poem which Goethe conceived and pondered upon very early in his life. He did not draft more than a few fragments of it, although in his autobiographical *Poetry And Truth* (translated by R. O. Moon), he tells fully how he had intended to treat it:

"I was now seized with the strange idea of treating epically the history of the Wandering Jew, which had long before been impressed on me by popular books, so as to bring out by means of this guide the prominent points of religious and Church history, as it should seem fit to me. But how I form the fable, and what meaning I put into it, I will now explain.

"In Jerusalem there was a shoemaker, to whom legend gives the name of Ahasuerus. For this character my Dresden shoemaker had given me the main features. I had fitted him out with the spirit and humour of a craftsman, of Hans Sachs, and ennobled him by an affection for Christ. As at the open workshop he liked to converse with the passers-by, teased them, and in Socratic fashion stimulated every one in his own way; neighbours and others among the people enjoyed lingering at his shop, even Pharisees and Sadducees spoke to him, and the Saviour Himself, accompanied by His disciples, would often stop by him. The shoemaker, whose thoughts were directed solely upon the work, conceived a special affection for our Lord, which was expressed for the most part by a desire to convert this lofty man, whose thoughts he did not comprehend, to his own way of thinking and acting. He therefore pressed upon him urgently to come out of His contemplation and not go about the country with such idlers, not to draw people away from their work into the desert. A people when assembled together, he said, was always excited, and no good would come of it.

"On the other hand, the Lord sought to instruct him by symbols in His higher views and aims, but these would not profit the sturdy man. Therefore, as Christ became more and more important, and, indeed, a public person, the benevolent craftsman expressed himself more sharply and vehemently, representing that disturbance and tumult would necessarily ensue, and Christ Himself would be compelled to declare Himself as head of a party, which could not possibly be His intention. When now the course of things followed, as we know them, Christ was taken and condemned; Ahasuerus was still more vehemently provoked when Judas, who had apparently betrayed the Lord, entered his workshop in despair, and with lamentations relates his unfortunate deed. He was, in fact, as well as the cleverest of the other disciples, firmly convinced that Christ would declare Himself regent and head of the nation. He had wished to compel the Lord, whose delay had hitherto been insuperable, by force to the deed, and therefore he had incited the priesthood to acts of violence which previously they had not dared to do. The disciples, on their side, were not without arms, and probably all would have turned out well, if the Lord had not given Himself up and left them in a most forlorn condition. Ahasuerus, who is not at all inclined to mildness by this narrative, embitters still more the condition of the poor ex-apostle, so that nothing remains for him but to hasten away and hang himself.

"Now, when Jesus was led to death past the workshop of the shoemaker, the well-known scene there took place. The sufferer sinks under the burden of the cross, and Simon of Cyrene is compelled to carry the same. Here Ahasuerus comes forth after the manner of men with hard intellect, who, when they see anyone suffering through their own fault, feel no pity, but are rather impelled by an untimely sense of justice to make matters worse by reproaches; he comes out and repeats all his former warnings, which he changes into violent accusations, and these his attachment to the sufferer seems to justify him in making. Christ does not answer, but at that instant the loving Veronica covers the face of the Saviour with the cloth; as she takes it away and raises it on high, Ahasuerus sees the countenance of the Lord upon it, but in no way that of the sufferer of the moment, but transfigured and shining with heavenly life. Blinded by this appearance, he turns away his eyes, and hears the words, 'Thou shalt wander over the earth until thou seest Me again in this form.' After some time, the man who is overwhelmed comes back to himself, finds that every one has pressed on to the place of execution; the streets of Jerusalem are deserted; restlessness and longing drive him forth, and he begins his wandering."

Thus, in Goethe's presentation, Ahasuerus becomes a symbol of Reason, and Jesus a symbol of Faith. Goethe planned to bring Ahasuerus together with Spinoza, the philosopher Goethe so greatly admired—but with what results we shall never know, since this episode was not drafted by Goethe.

The German poet Sigismund Heller produced a long poem in three parts entitled *The Wanderings of Ahasuerus*—an involved theological tract utilizing the story-structure of the legend. The motivation for the hositility of Ahasuerus takes a new form in this poem. Ahasuerus is presented as an ugly and deformed but very wealthy shoemaker, married to an exceedingly beautiful woman. Ahasuerus, a former schoolfellow of Jesus, turns into a bitter adversary when Jesus comes into a prominence which emphasizes his own obscurity, and he denounces Jesus as a dangerous impostor. One day Ahasuerus is told that Jesus and some of his Disciples have stopped to rest at his door, and Ahasuerus rushes out to warn them to move on and not to bring a curse on his household by touching his threshold. It is then that Jesus tells the shoemaker that the time will come when he will know Him. But it will take many generations before that day: "Nations shall come and go, but ye shall remain until the day of the last trumpet." Then follows a long and complicated recital, ending with a meeting between Ahasuerus and Luther.

Long epic poems have been written about the Wandering Jew in Polish and Russian literature. And in France, Pierre Dupont, inspired by Gustave Doré's drawings, wrote a long poem in 1856 to accompany them. The long poem is merely rhymed embroidery on the legend as presented in the imaginative drawings.

A more significant work appeared at the time Dupont's poem was published. It was a poem by Edouard Grenier, called *La mort du Juif errant* (*The Death of the Wandering Jew*). This poem enjoyed great popularity when first published because of its romantic qualities. Grenier describes the appearance of the Wandering Jew in the poet's hermitage, and gives the Wanderer's account of the agony of living on after all one loves—wife, children, friends—grow old and die.

A quarter of a century earlier, Edgar Quinet brought out a prose drama, *Ahasvérus,* which received great acclaim. The epic presented the universal tragedy of Man against God, and involved angels and demons and a considerable discussion of divine love. Quinet's epic influenced subsequent prose writers, notably Dumas, who used the figure of the Wandering Jew in their work.

Of all the French poems on this theme, the most popular was Pierre Jean de Béranger's *Ballad of the Wandering Jew*. The ballad was sung, at first, to ancient folk music, which was later superseded by music especially written for the ballad by Ernest Doré. Though the ballad loses much of its romantic appeal in translation, the following stanza from Béranger's poem may suggest the reason for its long popularity with the desperate masses of France bound to a fate from which they could not free themselves:

> For eighteen centuries, alas,
> O'er ashes of old Rome and Greece,
> O'er ruins of a thousand states,
> The whirlwind drove me from my peace.
> I've seen the good spring up and flower;
> I've seen great sorrows manifold;
> And from the parting waves arise
> Two worlds, successors of the old.
> Round, round,
> Grinds the world to which I'm bound,
> Round, round, round, round, round!

In English literature the legendary Wanderer was often used as a poetic symbol. In the work of the poet Shelley, this symbol looms large, and through it the poet expresses may of his ideas on tolerance, liberty, and the role of religion in human affairs. Shelley's interest in the legend began in 1809, when the poet was only seventeen or eighteen years old. At that time he wrote a story in collaboration with his cousin, Thomas Medwin. Then they turned the story, called *The Wandering Jew,* into a poem. The claim has been made that Shelley had come upon a copy of Schubart's *Rhapsody,* which made a deep impression upon him and suggested his own poem, which he was later to incorporate in *Queen Mab*—the poem that Shelley defended six years after its publication, but rejected before he died.

Though Shelley treated the Legend of the Wandering Jew in several of his poems, he used the symbol most completely and probingly in *Queen Mab*—in which Ahasuerus is presented as a Jewish Promethean character who defies the Lord and suffers perpetually but remains unrepentant. Unlike Job, who calls God to trial and to answer his accustions but in the end repents and abhors his own words, Ahasuerus continues to hold his head high in defiance to the end.

The poem *Queen Mab,* with its treatment of the Wandering Jew as a symbol of great protest and obdurate atheism, created a furor when the work first appeared.

After the dedication, the poem opens with the often-quoted lines that are a basic part of the theme:

> How wonderful is Death,
>   Death, and his brother Sleep:
> One, pale as yonder waning moon
>   With lips of lurid blue;
> The other, rosy as the morn
>   When throned on ocean's wave
>   It blushes o'er the world;
> Yet both so passing wonderful!

After some speculation on whether death is final or the soul sleeps on, the theme of the poem develops in a slow and complex reflection:

> "It is a wild and miserable world!
>   Thorny, and full of care,
>   Which every fiend can make his prey at will."

And in the course of the discussion, the Spirit of Ianthe, the central figure of the poem, recalls that during her

childhood her mother took her "to see an atheist burned."
When Ianthe cried, she was told:

> " 'Weep not, child!' cried my mother,
> 'for that man
>   Has said, There is no God.' "

The Fairy Mab deplores the fact that

>   "The name of God
>   Has fenced about all crime with holiness"

Then she declares to the Spirit of Ianthe:

> "These are my empire, for to me is given
> The wonders of the human world to keep,
> And Fancy's this creations to endow
> With manner, being, and reality;
> Therefore a wonderous phantom from the dreams
> Of human error's dense and purblind faith,
> I will evoke, to meet thy questioning.
> Ahasuerus, rise!"

And when Ahasuerus, "a strange and woe-worn wight"
rises, the Spirit asks him, "Is there a God?" Ahasuerus
pours out a torrent of defiance: "Is there a God:—ay,
an almighty God, and vengeful as almighty!" Then echoes
in his complaint the ancient indictment against the injustices of Fate.

>   "But my soul,
> From sight and sense of the polluting woe
> Of tyranny, had long learned to prefer
> Hell's freedom to the servitude of heaven.
> Therefore I rose, and dauntlessly began
> My lonely and unending pilgrimage,
> Resolved to wage unweariable war
> With my almighty tyrant, and to hurl
> Defiance at His impotence to harm,
> Beyond the curse I bore."

Here, then, we find Shelley portraying Ahasuerus as doomed to wander incessantly because of his unrepentant protest against the shackles of faith and the injustices to man by Fate; and he bears his doom or curse with "stubborn and unalterable will."

It is interesting to note that both Goethe's planned epic and Shelley's *Queen Mab* symbolize Ahasuerus as the man of reason pitted against God or Fate. But where Goethe extols Faith above Reason, and conceives of man's salvation as coming from the exploration of his own heart, Shelley prefers "Hell's freedom to the servitude of heaven."

Other English poets have tried to express through the tragedy of the Wanderer the tragedy of man upon this earth, seeking meaning and purpose and salvation but doomed to perpetual frustration. Wordsworth, in his *Song of the Wandering Jew,* laments:

> Day and night my toils redouble,
> Never nearer to the goal;
> Night and day, I feel the trouble
> Of the Wanderer in my soul.

Other poets, too, touched on the tragic plight of the Wanderer who, in essence, is the symbol of frustrated and often despairing mankind; but none explored it so fully, so passionately, and so defiantly as Shelley in his *Queen Mab*.

The unrepentant defiance of the Wanderer, developed by Shelley, is echoed in *The Curse of Immortality* by Eubule-Evans—a romantic dramatic poem, in which the Wanderer is called Theudas. He is doomed to wander until he repents, even if his repentance is only for a single moment. But like Shelley's Ahasuerus, Theudas proudly refuses to repent. Theudas cries out:

> "Twere mine
> To rest this moment in the sleep of death
> And how I yearn for it no heart can know:

> Would I but breathe one prayer of penitence.
> But this my nature knows not how to frame."

Theudas is doomed to wander, growing older as time goes by, but returning to the vigor of his youth every forty years. After sixteen centuries of stubborn challenge, love comes into his heart and leads Theudas to a state of grace. He falls in love with a girl named Leila, and together they enjoy the passing years, growing older together, their love giving forth "the mingled perfume of a joy which scents Existence far and wide." After forty years together Leila awakens one morning to discover that the sleeping Theudas is young again. She kisses him. He opens his eyes and calls her "mother," then falls asleep again. And she, in horror, realizing who he is, leaves him and throws herself into a lake. When Theudas learns what has happened, he prays for repentance. And

> In the furnace of sanctified joy,
> Earthly emotions are purged of alloy.

His long penance ended, he sinks down to the ground and dies.

2. The Legend in Fiction

As the Legend of the Wandering Jew began to wane as folklore, it suddenly and simultaneously inspired romantic novelists all over Europe to produce (within a quarter of a century or less) several scores of novels, most of them enormously long, and nearly all enjoying varying degrees of popularity. Most of the better novels on this theme were written between 1840 and 1860, and some of the novels which have appeared since were inspired by their predecessors in this field.

In a novel by Theodor Oelkers, *Princess Mary of Oldenhoff, or The Wandering Jew,* which was published in Leipzig in 1848, there are two improvisations on the legend not found in any other version: Ahasuerus is doomed to sacrifice whatever is dear to him in utter frustration, and he is given the fearful gift of foreseeing the future, so that he may know in advance all the dreadful things that will occur to him, and thus suffer the agony three times—in anticipation, in the event happening, and in remembrance of it through the centuries.

About three years later, Levin Schücking published his novel *The Peasant Prince,* which contains an episode, called "The Three Suitors." In this episode three strangers meet at an inn in Augsburg, in the year 1700. One of the strangers is a Dutch admiral, Van der Decken; one is a German nobleman, His Excellency the Master of Chase, Herr von Rodenstein; and the third is a young Armenian Prince, Isaac Laquedem. These three meet once every century to engage in revelry for a full year; then they part, each to assume his traditional role as Flying Dutchman, Wild Huntsman, and the Eternal Jew. During this particular meeting, the three engage in a great deal of mischief in quiet Augsburg. In the course of their stay they meet a beautiful but haughty woman, and all three try to win and subdue her. What follows is the meat and plot of the episode in the novel. The book was quite popular in its day, and may have influenced a novel written in the United States about a century later, called *My First Two Thousand Years,* by George Sylvester Viereck and Paul Eldridge—in which Laquedem gives full range to the amatory talents attributed him by Schücking.

A number of novelists in Germany after Oelkers and Schücking used the theme of the Wandering Jew in their work; and, apparently, there were others before them. For Goethe records that he planned his epic poem on the theme, "which had long before been impressed on me by popular books."

Denmark's most notable contribution in literature on the legend is *Ahasuerus* by the beloved fairy-tale writer, Hans Christian Andersen. Andersen presents Ahasuerus as the Angel of Doubt, who was born as a human being in the same hour in which Jesus was born—so that Faith and Doubt came to mankind simultaneously. Ahasuerus grows up to become a shoemaker in Jerusalem, a man wise and witty and well liked by his neighbors. Many gather in his workshop to hear his clever discourses. Children come to hear his stories; and learned men come to engage him in discussion. Among his growing audience of listeners is young Veronica, who has recently become enchanted by a new prophet from Nazareth. Another frequenter of Ahasuerus' workshop is a recent disciple of the Nazarene, named Judas. Ahasuerus pours out his wrathful doubt upon the heads of all the false prophets; and his convincing talk infects Judas with doubt until he decides to test Jesus and find out whether he is really the Messiah. If Jesus is really the Son of Man, so Judas in his tormented mind argues, then the hosts of heaven will come to assist him. Judas, according to this version, instigated by the arguments of the Angel of Doubt, betrays Jesus only that Jesus may prove His power. When Jesus consents to be made a prisoner and later dies on the Cross, Judas commits suicide; and Ahasuerus the Doubter begins to wander over the earth to spread heresy and disbelief. He witnesses the burning pyres that consume the Christian martyrs, Veronica among them. But as time passes, Ahasuerus sees the gradual rooting of Christianity in the world. Ahasuerus, the Angel of Doubt, continues his wanderings throughout the centuries, as a symbol of defiance to all that is divine. Andersen follows Ahasuerus on his many adventures and finally brings him, with Columbus, to the New World. And here, in the New World, the Angel of Doubt gains

Belief—and then comes the time for him to return to his place in heaven.

Thus Andersen makes Ahasuerus the symbol of all men of little faith whose doom is brought about by doubt and denial of God, and whose redemption comes from belief.

About the same time the legend was generally being adapted by novelists in Germany, Denmark, Poland and the Low Countries, two novels appeared in France that created a sensation and were eagerly read in translation throughout Europe and America for nearly a century.

One of these novels was *Tarry Till I Come: or The Everlasting Jew* by Alexander Dumas. It was natural for the author of *The Three Musketeers* and *The Count of Monte Cristo* to be intrigued by the tales current in his day about Isaac Laquedem (Lakedion or Lakadama), a soldier of Pilate's court, cursed with immortality. In all likelihood he had read novels and stories about the Wanderer popular in Europe at that time and the legend seemed peculiarly suited for a romantic novel in the Dumas manner.

Dumas (unlike most of his novelist predecessors and successors coping with this theme) condensed the action in his novel to a brief period, beginning in the year 1471, and restricted the major events to a few days preceding and following Holy Thursday in that year. And he introduced a new motivation for Laquedem's original antagonism to Jesus.

The setting of the novel is Rome in the year 1471. Thousands of pilgrims are coming into the Holy City to receive the blessing of Pope Paul II on Holy Thursday. In a crowd streaming toward the city there is a stranger about forty years of age, of medium height and sturdy build, his sorrowful face burned by sun and wind. He wears bleached and worn garments of a fashion difficult to identify, and walks with the steady plodding gait of one accustomed to long journeys on foot. He is sunk in contemplation, speaking only when spoken to, and often his replies are puzzling, for he speaks as one who remembers times long past.

As they near the Holy City, the stranger startles his traveling companions by parting from them to take a short-cut past strongholds and over roads forbidden to trespassers at the pain of death. The stranger overcomes a succession of obstacles by his unequaled skill in archery and his uncanny knowledge of the past, and, finally, when the soldiers of one fort let fly a barrage of arrows at the trespasser, they glanced off his cloak and fall to the ground, and he goes on unscathed.

In Rome the stranger finds a place in the crowd where he can see the Pope and hear the blessing. Later, in the Benediction Room, when the Pope washes the feet of thirteen pilgrims, according to the tradition, the stranger is the last of the thirteen. As the Pope performs the rite, the stranger prostrates himself and begs the Holy Father to hear his confession. The Pope grants his wish. And later, when the stranger comes to the Venice Palace for confession, the Pope tries to assure him in advance that the mercy of the All-Merciful is great enough to forgive any misdeed.

"I am the man who had no pity before the Great Sorrow," the stranger begins his confession. "I am he who refused one minute of repose at my door to the Son of Man!"

His name, he tells the Pope, is Isaac Lakadama, and he was a soldier who served the Procurator of Judaea in the days when Jesus was on trial. Before he went into the service of Pilate he had been a soldier with Quintilius Varus and had taken part in the battles of Bructeraea, in which the Romans suffered a humiliating defeat and their proud standards were trampled underfoot. When Jesus came before Pilate and the eagle standards bowed down in salutation, he, Lakadama, still remembering the humiliation at Bructeraea, came forward and offered to test the proud Roman standards again. He stood firmly bearing his standard, but as Jesus advanced, the eagle inclined to the ground, bowing Lakadama with it until he was almost prostrate. Then it was that he conceived his great bitterness toward Jesus, whom he accused of being a false prophet. Later, when Jesus was led to Golgotha, Lakadama with his wife and son and daughter climbed a stone bench in front of their home to watch the procession. And Jesus stumbled near the bench. Jesus asked Lakadama to hand out his stool that Jesus might rest. And Lakadama replied: "No; tarry not before my house, but go on." Then his doom was pronounced in the reply by Jesus: "It is you who must tarry while others know rest. You shall travel forever."

The stranger goes on to relate that his family and his home were destroyed by a storm that night, and he then started on his endless travels. In his longing for death he attempted to end his life by flinging himself into the crater of Vesuvius, by hurling himself from a precipice into the raging sea, by walking into consuming forest fires, by entering the dens of wild animals—but he could not die.

Now, after fourteen centuries of wandering and suffering, he begs the Pope to intercede for him so that he may die.

What follows is a complicated story woven about the Pope's promise to pray for Lakadama that very night. The Pope is found dead the next morning, but in his right hand he clenches a chrysolite containing one drop of water from Lethe. Lakadama alone can unclench the Pope's hand, and he drinks the drop of water. At once he is back in Jerusalem, beseeching Another to allow him to rest, and the Other extends his arms in help. Then Lakadama cries out: "No, Lord, I am not worthy of Thy mercy. Honor instead of me the man who laid down his life for Thy last enemy."

The long and intricate novel cannot be condensed into so brief a synopsis, but this brief sketch indicates how Dumas coped with the origin of Lakadama's guilt through his sin of pride, and its resolution in the end through his repentance.

A more lastingly popular novel on this theme came from the author of *The Mysteries of Paris*—Eugène Sue. As soon as his novel *The Wandering Jew*, appeared in 1844, a storm of bitter controversy arose that did not subside for a long time. Sue's novel is a monument to his creative ability, for it held a large following of readers spellbound through twelve hundred pages of blood and thunder against the social abuses of his time.

The legendary figure, from which the novel derives its title, actually plays a minor role in the book, as a symbol of restless and exploited humanity.

The main theme of Sue's novel is man's inhumanity to man, although along the way he pauses to explore abuses in various institutions. All his ideas are framed within a triple concept of immortality: The immortality of the family; the immortality of property, represented by money; and the immortality of the organization or association. A man can become immortal in the successive chain of his family; in the continuity of his money that increases through interest by the mere passing of time; and through becoming part of a company, an association, or an organization which continues to have a life of its own though individuals in it may pass away. The immortality of the family, according to this novel, conflicts with the immortality of money which thrives by interest (considered evil and prohibited in ancient times, when all forms of interest were treated as usury); and the immortality of the organization (represented by the Jesuits in Sue's novel) comes into conflict with the interests of the family in their claim to the rights in family property.

With this theme constantly in the background, Sue presents a gargantuan clash between the interests of these three entities, and uses the device of having the family represented by the Wandering Jew in a complex plot that gives the author ample scope in which to elaborate on his many social theories and on many of his personal prejudices—particularly against the Jesuits—which were the primary cause of the bitter criticism when the novel first appeared.

Other French novels on the Wanderer appeared, but none were as original or as popular as those by Dumas and Sue. In the same period novelists elsewhere built upon the elements of the legend a great variety of fictional structures, each according to his talents and inclinations.

Almost two decades before the novels of Dumas and Sue appeared in France, and the novel by Oelkers in Germany, an anonymous prose fantasy appeared in England called *Salathiel: A Story of the Past, the Present and the Future*. In subsequent editions the authorship of this work in three volumes, published in 1827, was credited to the Reverend George Croly, who used the legend as a fictional tool to carve a monumental homily on Protestantism in general, and on Lutheranism, in particular. The book was fairly popular for a number of years. In America it appeared under the title, *Salathiel or Tarry Thou till I Come!* and also under the abbreviated title of *Tarry Thou till I Come!"*

These are a few of the better known of the many novels based upon the legend in nineteenth-century literature. Since that time fiction writers have often referred to the Legend of the Wanderer in their works or used it as a variation on a theme of their own. Maxwell Sommerville, the Scottish novelist—and son of a Scottish poet—wrote a novel, *The Wanderer's Legend,* published in London in 1902, which dealt with the Wandering Jew.

And a year later O. Henry wrote a short story in the typical O. Henry manner, called *The Door of Unrest* which nevertheless reflected the change in approach to the legend from the intensely theological to the psychological. The story, told in the first person, presents the new editor of the Montopolis *Weekly Bugle,* at the end of a day in his office, working on an editorial and wondering "what Mrs. Flanagan was going to have for supper," when, in the twilight, "Father Time's younger brother" drifts into the office and perches himself on the corner of the desk. The stranger introduces himself as *"Michob Ader"* (*the* Michob Ader of the Turkish Spy report, a shoemaker who lived during the days of the Crucifixion). When the editor mutters that his visitor must be the Wandering Jew, Michob Ader retorts bitterly: " 'Tis a lie, like nine tenths of what ye call history. 'Tis a Gentile I am, and no Jew." Then he talks about Ptolemy the Great, tries to straighten out the editor on events occurring in the days of Nero, gives the true site of Solomon's Temple, and describes "the little man," Tamerlane, buried in Samarkand.

As might be expected in an O. Henry story, the editor discovers the following day that his visitor Michob Ader is none other than the Montopolis shoemaker Mike O'Bader, who, when inebriated, goes around informing everyone that he is the Wandering Jew—though he insists the Wandering Jew is a Gentile. How Mike O'Bader came to be that way and in his cups suffers from great guilt gives to the end of the story the famous O. Henry twist.

Among more recent novels and short stories on the legend, *My First Two Thousand Years* by Viereck and Eldridge, and Edmond Fleg's *Jesus: Told by the Wandering Jew*, have received the widest attention—for opposite reasons.

My First Two Thousand Years, by George Sylvester Viereck and Paul Eldridge, was published in 1928 in New York and was soon translated into German to the delight of all embryonic Nazis. The long book, exceedingly well written for its genre, has an intriguing plot, beginning with the American Professors Lowell and Bassermann in a monastery near Mount Athos, when they meet a mysterious Mr. Laquedem and his Oriental valet Kotikokura. In the course of their first conversation, Laquedem tells Bassermann that he remembers him as a

Disciple of Jesus, and that his name at that time was Saint Thomas. From there on, in an on-the-spot fashion, we glimpse through Laquedem's eyes the highlights of events through almost two thousand years of history which, according to these authors, took place principally in scented boudoirs.

Quite a different book is Edmond Fleg's *Jesus*. Instead of using titillation, Fleg soberly probes for an answer to a profound age-old question: How can the teaching of Jesus be equated with the actions of Christians, particularly in such periods as the Crusades and the Inquisition. Fleg's narrative is eloquent, and his approach to Jesus humbly reverent, as a Jew toward a great Jewish prophet —since in the days of Jesus there was no other measure. Though written with enticing devices, the work is less a novel or a fictionized Life of Jesus, and more a retelling of the story of Jesus as given in the New Testament Gospels and in the Apocryphal Gospels, with a running commentary by Edmond Fleg. He uses the device of the Wandering Jew, who is a man paralyzed from birth and made to walk again by one word from the Nazarene. And yet when Jesus stumbled on his way to Golgotha and called out to the man he had healed, "Carry my cross!" there was no answer or help; and the blessing the man had received through the cure of his paralysis became his curse—to walk and wander until Jesus comes again. He wanders down the ages from Tiberius to Justinian, from Mohammed to Luther, and from Tamerlane to President Lebrun. And Fleg's novel might well be the definitive footnote to the entire Christological exploration of the Legend of the Wandering Jew.

3. The Legend in Music and Art

CONSIDERING how stimulating the Legend of the Wandering Jew proved in literature, it is astonishing how slight its influence was in music and art.

Many early ballads on this theme were sung to existing folk tunes. There is only one ballad or poem, that of Béranger (also first sung to the tune of an ancient folk song), which was later set to a new air especially composed for it by Ernest Doré.

Some writers erroneously credit a distinguished grand opera as devoted to the theme of the Wanderer—*La Juive* (*The Jewess*) by Jacques Halévy, with libretto by Augustin Scribe. The confusion arose quite naturally. Halévy (1799-1862), father-in-law of Georges Bizet, was the composer of forty-four comic and serious operas. The most successful of these was *La Juive*, which he composed at the age of thirty five, and which was first presented in Paris in 1835. Subsequently it was performed in every operahouse in the world, and it is still occasionally presented. *La Juive* is a melodramatic opera, unrelieved by lighter touches, dealing with race hatred and mob violence in the Middle Ages against Eleazar, a Jewish merchant, and his beautiful daughter. A man pretending to be a Jew falls in love with the girl, and she with him. Later it is discovered that he is a Christian nobleman, and married. The nobleman is banished, and the merchant and his daughter are sent to the gallows. When it is too late to save the father and daughter from execution, it is learned that the girl was a Christian child the merchant rescued in infancy and raised as his own.

This solitary opera, the only one dealing with a Jewish-persecution theme, became intimately identified with Halévy.

Nearly a quarter of a century after *La Juive* was written, Halévy, just four years before his death, apparently composed the music for an opera using the Legend of the Wandering Jew, based on a libretto by Scribe and Saint-Georges. The opera was apparently never performed. Though it is sometimes mentioned by writers on the Wandering Jew, it is not listed in the standard records of the works by either Halévy or Scribe. Paul Lacroix, in the Bibliographical Notice preceding Gustave Doré's illustrations of the Legend of the Wandering Jew (in the Addey, 1857 edition) writes: "No less than ten French pieces bear his [the Wandering Jew's] name—from the melodrama of Caignez [sic], played at La Gaieté in 1812, up to the grand opera of MM. Scribe and Saint-Georges, set to music by M. Halévy, at the Imperial Academy of Music, 1852."

One can readily see how the two operas by the same composer and librettist, dealing with a closely related theme became fused or confused.

As in music, so also in art, there are few distinguished works—and only one really outstanding contribution—inspired by the legend.

The Wanderer was one of the oldest subjects of wood engravings, and some existed as early as the seventeenth century, when reports of the appearance of the Wandering Jew began to circulate. Later there were ballads and (still later) novels that contained imaginative illustrations.

The most noteworthy illustrations on the theme are Gustave Doré's twelve wood engravings of *The Legend of the Wandering Jew* that have appeared in various editions.

The engravings begin with a scene at the foot of Golgotha where Jesus, in the center of a great crowd, pronounces the curse on the shoemaker in the shadowed foreground. A series of ten engravings follow, presenting the harassed and aged Wanderer during the following centuries: on a desolate road in a downpour; passing through Brussels; leaving a Flemish inn; fording a river in a deserted and awesome area; in a French graveyard; in a Swiss valley; climbing the peaks of snow-capped mountains; coming into a town under attack by a medieval army; shipwrecked in a raging sea; crossing the Andes. The last illustration shows the release of the Wanderer in a macabre setting, with a trumpet sounding in the sky to shake the earth to its foundations, in which, at last, the Wanderer sits down, puts his staff away, and takes off his Wanderer's shoes.

4. The Legend in Drama

IN no field has the Legend of the Wanderer been so effectively used as in the drama, in which it has been made a vehicle to convey varied ideas. Curiously enough, though a few plays had been written in the eighteenth and the nineteenth centuries on this theme, a larger number appeared early in our own century.

The first available drama produced on the stage that makes oblique use of the legend was a comedy presented in England in 1797. In 1812 at La Gaieté in Paris a melodrama was presented, by Caigniez, which exploited the theme of the Wandering Jew. And in 1827 the German dramatist, August Klingemann produced his play in five acts, *Ahasver*, based on Franz Horn's novel *The*

Eternal Jew, which had been published about a decade earlier. A few years later (1834) Vincent Victor Joly's three-act play *Le Juif errant* was produced in Paris. And a few other less distinguished plays were produced on the same theme before the century was over.

But it was not until early in the twentieth century that a number of plays on the theme of the Wanderer appeared in quick succession. Frido Grelle's poetic drama in three acts, *Ahasver: der ewige Kampf!,* appeared in 1919; David Mackinnon's *Ahasuerus: A Persian Play,* was produced in London in 1920; Wilhelm Gruendler's *Ahasuerus,* a tragedy in five acts, was produced in Germany in 1928; in 1929 Charles E. Lawrence wrote his one-act *Spikenard,* based on the legend; in Paris, Maxime Alexandre produced in 1946 his three-act play, *Le Juif errant*; and there were a number of other plays in German, French and English which appeared in between, each giving a different mood, each exploring a different aspect of the legend.

How the treatment of the theme in drama differed from its treatment in poetry or fiction (apart from the difference in approach inherent in the medium) may perhaps be indicated by a synopsis of a few of these plays, ranging from the earliest play available to us, to the last successful play on the topic.

THE WANDERING JEW, OR LOVE'S MASQUERADE

One would expect that the story of a man who becomes rejuvenated every forty or seventy years, and who has had experiences the world over, would lend itself to humorous as well as dramatic situations. But singularly few humorous works have been produced. The first play on the topic, however, called: *The Wandering Jew, or Love's Masquerade,* is a comedy in two acts, which was produced at the Theatre-Royal in Drury Lane, London, in 1797.

This comedy is a farcical contrivance, for which the following apology is offered in the *Prologue:*

> In former times the prologue, we are told,
> Would all the mystery of the plot unfold;
> But modern poets, wiser far than they,
> With care conceal the plot of every play;
> So close and long they keep it—cunning elves!
> You'd almost swear 'twas hidden from themselves.
>   Just so our Bard; as sly, withholds the clue,
> And leaves it all to fortune and to you.
> If plot you find, he hopes you will not scout it;
> If none you find, he hopes you'll do without it.

The plot concerns grumpy Sir Solomon Swallow, guardian of his niece Camilla, who is the same age as his daughter Lydia—both of whom are at the age of romance. The girls are courted by, and very much in love with, two young men, Major Atall and Captain Marall. Sir Solomon, aware of his niece's infatuation, disapproves of her young man so violently that he vows to give her in marriage to the oldest man to be found in England.

Captain Marall, Camilla's suitor, with the aid of Major Atall, contrives to insert a notice in the newspapers that the Wandering Jew, named Mr. Mathuzalem, and his inseparable servant-companion, Juba ("within a century or two as old as himself"), have returned to visit London; and that Mathuzalem intends to marry a British girl "by whom he may leave an heir to his wealth and his longevity." This item attracts Sir Solomon's attention, and he immediately invites Mathuzalem and his companion to his mansion. And he is determined to offer his niece in marriage to Mathuzalem.

The two young suitors in their disguises arrive promptly, and garrulous Captain Marall, disguised as Juba, to impress Sir Solomon with his master's age, recalls in detail the time that he and Mathuzalem last dined in London with Julius Caesar and the time when, they dined weekly with Michelangelo. In spite of Mathuzalem's efforts to stem his companion's torrent of fantastic reminiscences, Juba goes on to recall events, such as the time Mathuzalem was asked to be godfather at the christening of Remus and Romulus, and the time he traveled through Egypt with St. Patrick and picked up from him "a slight smack of the brogue."

The masqueraders are finally exposed. But by then Sir Solomon relents and grants the two young ladies permission to marry the young men they love.

Love's Masquerade, whatever else it may prove or disprove, shows that at the end of the eighteenth century the Legend of the Wandering Jew was sufficiently known in England to be familiar to a theater audience, even in farcical disguise.

THE ETERNAL JEW

In Jewish folklore the Wanderer is personified in Elijah the Prophet, often called the "immortal" and sometimes the "eternal" Jew. Though Elijah has been commemorated in numerous stories and legends both in Hebrew and in Yiddish literature, the only play treating the legend of the Wanderer in which he is not Elijah the Prophet is a one-act play, *The Eternal Jew*, written in 1906 by the well-known Yiddish dramatist, David Pinski. The play was translated into English in 1920 by Isaac Goldberg, under the title *The Stranger*. But by that time it had already been made famous in its Hebrew translation, as presented by the experimental group theater Habima.

Raikin Ben-Ari, one of the original members of this theatrical group, in his book, *Habima*, which records the formation, the trials and tribulations of this theater group in Russia and elsewhere, explains the instant success of Pinski's one-act, and how its mystical message electrified audiences.

The play is a dramatization of an almost two-thousand-year-old legend found in the great commentary (the *Midrash Rabbah*) on the Biblical Book of Lamentations. And this is the midrashic legend:

In the days when the Romans were besieging Jerusalem (70 A.D.), a Jewish farmer in Galilee was plowing in the field one day when one of his oxen stopped in the furrow and began to bellow mournfully. The farmer was about to strike the animal and urge it to move on when an old Arab with a snow-white beard appeared before him and commanded him not to strike the ox.

"Who are you?" asked the farmer.

The stranger disregarded his question and said: "If you are a Jew, unyoke the oxen and stop your work, for at this very moment the Holy Temple in Jerusalem is being destroyed."

"How do you know that?" asked the farmer.

"I know it by the bellowing of your animal."

But as the farmer was unyoking his animals, one of the oxen bellowed again. And the stranger said: "Put your oxen back into harness and return to your work, for at this moment the Redeemer of Israel was born."

"What is his name?" asked the farmer in awe, realizing now that he stood before a messenger of God.

"His name is Menahem—the Consoler; and his father's name is Hezekiah; and he dwells in the Arab section of Bethlehem in Judah," answered the stranger. Whereupon he disappeared.

Then the farmer took his oxen in their harness to the marketplace and sold them; and with the money he bought fine linen for swaddling clothes, and set out to wander from village to village, looking for the Messiah's mother. When he came to Bethlehem, many women in the village clustered about to buy his linen, but the mother of the child Menahem did not buy any.

The farmer said to her: "Why don't you buy linen for your child?"

And she answered: "Because my child is a child of sorrow, for he was born on the day the Holy Temple was destroyed."

Whereupon the farmer said to her: "We must place our trust in the Lord! Through him was the Temple destroyed and through him it will be rebuilt. Now, take the linen for your child, and in the days to come I will return for the money."

So she took the linen and went her way.

Some days later he returned to Bethlehem in Judah and asked after the child. And the mother said: "Did I not tell you that he was a child of sorrow and his fate an evil one? For since you were here, great storms arose and carried him away, and I cannot find him."

The farmer then said to her: "Did I not tell you that through him the Temple was destroyed and through him it would be rebuilt?"

In Pinski's play, the stranger, representing the farmer-prophet, tells his listeners in the marketplace: "Yes, I am a sinner. I have committed the greatest sin. For I was plowing my field when I should have been taking part in the struggle for the freedom of my people. Now God's terrible punishment is upon me. I shall have to wander all over the world, and long, long shall I seek the Messiah. Now I go to do what I must—what I must."

Ben-Ari, in his book, reports: "I can still see Zemach [the actor who took the part of the farmer-prophet] before me, lifting his bag and staff with a piercing sigh, climbing up to the top of the construction, where he exclaimed in a mystic tone of voice: *Ani holech le-happes et ha-mashiah!* [I am going in search of the Messiah!]." Those were not empty words for him. He was always looking for a Messiah for himself, for the theatre, for the people. He believed in the redemption of his people and hoped that the Habima would bring the problem of the Jew before the eyes of the world, and thus contribute toward this redemption by acquainting the world with the real hopes and aspirations of the Jew."

It is reported that the great Russian writer, Maxim Gorki, attended the Habima performance of Pinski's *The*

Eternal Jew several times; and though he did not understand a word of Hebrew, he was deeply moved by the tragic grandeur of its theme.

David Pinski had taken a very old legend and dramatically underscored its sin-and-redemption theme.

THE WANDERING JEW

The most popular play so far on the theme of the Wanderer has been *The Wandering Jew: A Play in Four Phases,* by E. Temple Thurston, which was first produced successfully in London in 1920, and has since been repeatedly produced both in England and in the United States.

The play begins with a Crier calling out to the audience in a darkened hall before the curtain rises: "To each his destiny—to each his Fate. We are wanderers in a foreign land between the furrow and the stars."

The first "phase" follows the traditional Protestant version of the legend, excepting that it gives a new motivation for the Wanderer-to-be, named Matathias, for his resentment of Jesus. Matathias, who is the same age as Jesus, is in love with and lives with a woman he has taken away from her husband and child, and the woman has become ill through unbearable longing for her child. She implores Matathias to ask the Nazarene Healer to help her. At first, because of his guilt-ridden conscience, Matathias refuses to approach Jesus; but later, when her condition grows critical, Matathias asks Jesus to come and heal her. Jesus replies: "Return the woman to her husband and she shall be healed." It is then that Matathias conceives his bitter resentment toward the Nazarene. Later, when Jesus is led to Golgotha, Matathias spits in the face of Jesus and urges him on; and Jesus then pronounces upon Matathias the curse to wander over the earth until the Second Coming.

In the second "phase," during the tenth century, the Wandering Matathias takes part in a joust in which he is victorious, since he cannot die. But he is not so successful in his passionate love of Lady de Beaudricourt. The third "phase" takes place nearly three centuries later, when Matathias is abandoned by his wife, who had changed her faith to marry him, to become a nun after their only child is killed—for she assumes she has been punished for abandoning the Church and having married a Jew. The fourth "phase" takes place in Seville where Matathias, now a physician, is brought before the Inquisition, and when it is discovered that he is a Jew, he is condemned to die. When Matathias (now called Matteos) is offered mercy by the tribunal of the Inquisition, the accused wants to know the price of this mercy. "Declare here now the faith of Holy Mother Church. . . . declare you were a Jew on whom the light of this our Christian faith had fallen," he is told. Matteos refuses the offer, and replies: "The Spirit of your Christ is nearer to my heart as I stand here—a Jew—than it could be to those who would so thrust Him 'tween their lips."

Later Matteos is placed at the stake, and a bright light falls on his figure as the flames go up. And the Crier finally calls out: "Matteos Buttadios, the Jew, is dead."

THE IMMORTAL JEW

If an award were offered to the most probing use of the theme of the Wanderer in dramatic form, it would probably go to *The Immortal Jew,* a drama in three acts, by the English poet, Sidney Royce Lysaght. The play was first published in 1931, and it, too, seems to have been presented on the stage.

In this play, covering about a century, the Wandering Jew is not a Jew; and he is also not physically immortal. He lives and dies quite normally. But his immortal soul is transmigrated, generation after generation, retaining and regretting the same basic human weaknesses that plague his conscience. He differs from other people in just one respect: in times of crises, when his conscience comes into strong conflict with his temporal passions, he suddenly remembers similar situations and conflicts between his head and his heart, between his reason and his passion, in former incarnations, going back and back, century after century.

The play begins on a Christmas eve, A.D. 1820, in the churchyard of the village of Rosenberg in Bohemia, where a tall, bearded, travel-stained and noble-appearing man of about sixty wanders among the tombstones, reading the epitaphs and listening to the voices of a children's choir coming from the church nearby, singing: "One for Peter, two for Paul, A threepenny loaf will serve us all." As the stranger meditates, a benign and gentle priest, Father Marck, comes out of the church, and the stranger addresses him by name, amazing the priest with his knowledge of affairs in the castle of Count Skala, Lord of Rosenberg. Then the stranger asks after the child, son of Ambrose Skala, Jr., left in the priest's care by the mother when the child's father died. The stranger reveals himself as Ambrose Skala, Sr., grandfather of the child, who had rejected his son and now wishes to leave money with the priest for his grandson's education. In the course of their conversation, Ambrose recalls events of three centuries earlier; and when Father Marck tries to correct him and says he must be talking of events that had happened in the days of his great-grandparents, the man replies:

> "We are our own forefathers! He who seeks
> Excuse in the hereditary stain
> For his misdeeds condemns himself alone.
> He was that very man whose sin began
> The stain that tarnishes his reborn soul!"

Lysaght comes back again and again to his basic concept that:

> "You are your own forefathers, and begetters

> Of all the ills that hold your souls in fetters.
> To love thy neighbor as thyself were wise,
> Because he is thyself in disguise.
> Each is the keeper of the other's life,
> Or else the robber of the other's store;
> And when thou liest with the neighbor's wife
> Thou art the cuckold and thy wife the whore."

The conversation between Father Marck and Ambrose Skala is interrupted by the children coming out of the church, singing. The priest turns to them; and when he looks again toward Ambrose, the stranger is gone. "It is nearly dark, and the wind is loud in the forest trees."

Twenty years later Ambrose Skala, the child reared by Father Marck, is twenty-two years old and prepared to go to Prague to further his education. Karel Tomek, his closest friend, comes to say farewell and confides in Ambrose that he is in love with Mila, Father Marck's niece. When Tomek departs and Mila arrives to take leave of Ambrose, he makes love to her and arranges to meet her that evening in the garden. This clandestine affair is carried on for several years, even after Mila has married Karel, and ends with Mila's suicide.

Nearly three-quarters of a century later, during World War I, we find the young poet-dramatist Stefan Skala, a descendant of Ambrose Skala, embroiled in a betrayal, different in circumstance but the same in essence; and he acts in accord with his inherited nature, realizing that

> "The choice between the yea and nay,
> In moments when I know I have the power
> To shape my course, or drift along the tide,
> That choice is Me;—all else is ancestry."

Lysaght's play is so compactly planned and structured that its profundity and dramatic excitement become impossible to convey in a brief digest.

The four plays, *Love's Masquerade*, *The Eternal Jew*, *The Wandering Jew*, and *The Immortal Jew*—even in their titles—suggest the diversity of thesis and treatment to which the theme of the Wandering Jew lends itself, and which is turned into ever-new forms by the creative dramatist.

5. The Legend in Films

THE first film to treat the legend, according to the *Motion Picture World* of July, 1915, was produced in 1913 by Roma-America—a silent film based upon Eugène Sue's novel; and its reception has not been traceably recorded. Ten years later, another attempt was made by Stoll in England, and this time the film was based on E. Temple Thurston's play. From records available, this film made no greater impression than its predecessor. A decade later, in 1933, Jaffa Productions released a film in Yiddish, entitled: *The Wandering Jew* and starring the distinguished actor, Jacob Ben-Ami. This film, shown in New York at the RKO Cameo Theatre, received little attention. There may have been others. But all the early films on this theme seemed never to have passed through the glare of fame or even notoriety.

In 1934–1935 Twickenham Studios in England produced an ambitious film based on Thurston's play which starred the German actor, Conrad Veidt. In England it was distributed by Gaumont-British Films; and in the United States by Olympic Pictures. But the timing was unfortunate. For at the time the picture was released, tempers were strained by strident Nazi propaganda, in general, and its scurrilous attack on Jews, in particular; and protests arose from many quarters. The film was soon withdrawn or buried by failure.

After World War II, Distributori Independenti in Italy produced a film in 1948 under Goffred Allessandri's direction, starring Vittorio Gassman, and called, at first, *L'ebrero errante* (*The Wandering Jew*), the title later changed to *Sabbie del tempo* (*The Sands of Time*). This was a dramatization of the plight of the Jews under Naziism, and depicted the fate of a group of Jews arrested in Paris under the German occupation and sent to a concentration camp in Germany. The moral strength of the prisoners under the degrading and inhuman Nazi treatment symbolized the triumph of their immortal souls. This film, with English captions, was released in the United States by Globe Films under the title of *The Sands of Time,* and attained a fair success. It was later distributed by President Film Distributors; and, in sixteen millimeter, it is still available through Brandon Films.

However, none of the films up to that point probed deeply into the rich theme, or produced a motion picture of epic proportions.

Part Four

SO THE LEGEND
ENDS

N ow the legend has come full circle.

The legend we have briefly probed, examining its roots and its influence on literature, is, quite obviously, of ancient origin. It is older than Christianity or even recorded history; its beginnings date back to the time when man first developed a conscience.

How long ago this happened, measured in time, is difficult even to guess at; yet how it happened we can learn from the mores and traditions of communities still in existence which have retained all the characteristics of prehistoric peoples. For the evolution of social organization never took place along a single progressive and unified line. Civilization developed sooner with some and later with others. Some started on the road to civilization and for reasons unknown retrogressed and sank back into a more primitive state or were lost. Some jumped great gaps. And some, for a number of reasons, never got started. So that even today, in our atomic age, there are still isolated communities—in the jungles of Australia, in remote Melanesian islands, the Malay Archipelago, and others—where life approximates prehistoric modes. And a study of their traditions, taboos, and legends reveals the rise of basic concepts, mental attitudes, fears and hopes found in our own society, though ours appear cloaked in new terms and bearing new symbolic meanings. The study of the taboos and mores of such primitive people clarifies our understanding of the origin of conscience, which in its earliest form was a conscious conflict in the mind of man between the desire to do something forbidden by a prohibition or taboo, and the desire to conform to the authority of such a societal prohibition or taboo. Conscience developed in the conflict between man's desires and their frustration by communal strictures or laws.

Social strictures and divine prohibitions, by their very nature, imply conflict; for what is prohibited is what man in a natural state would desire and instinctively wish to do. When we find in all early societies the bitterest taboo against incest, it is proof that this was prevalent in an earlier period; when we find the commandment against murder, it verifies that the desire to kill lurked deep in the human animal; and when, in much more developed societies, we find the commandment to honor and care for the aged, it clearly indicates that the young tended to abandon the old. This implication lies within every social or religious prohibition, taboo or commandment.

With the appearance of restrictions and taboos arose conflict. And with the appearance of the individual's revolt against authority arose the sense of guilt. When a man revolted against the authority of a law or taboo, and committed an act counter to tribal or communal law, he had committed a *crime,* and if discovered, he was punished. This was from the start the simple pattern of crime and punishment. But when a man revolted in thought—feeling the urge to murder, or steal, or covet his neighbor's wife, or to do any one of a thousand things he desired to do which were prohibited—or if he committed such an act without being discovered, he knew he had committed a *sin.* And his conscience plagued him. For he felt guilty. He could know no peace of mind unless he were cleansed of his guilt. The first stage of contrition, or regret, led the contrite to try to cleanse themselves through self-imposed punishment.

The authority against which people in a primitive society revolted often became symbolized in the father or Father. The revolt, in deed or thought, was the sin;

the sense of guilt was contrition; the punishment self-imposed to pay for the sin, was the way of penance; and the goal was peace of mind, or redemption.

In his natural state, we assume man lived in accord with his own nature, without conflict in his own mind and heart. He lived then in the mythical state in which there is no guilt. But as soon as he entered societal organization, of necessity regulated by taboos and laws, he was driven from his earthly paradise and became the eternal wanderer, restlessly searching for an escape from his guilt.

Though this is a great oversimplification of the exceedingly complex topic of guilt, it may give a glimpse of the background against which early man struggled with the problem of conscience, which he began to symbolize and depict in the Legend of the Wanderer.

In every culture and in every religion a legend of the Wanderer appears, assuming in each, new symbols and new forms, molded by the characteristic beliefs of each culture. But in them all we find the cycle of the Wanderer progressing from guilt to repentance, from repentance to penance, from penance to ultimate redemption.

In Greek mythology there are a number of myths on the theme of man's revolt against authority, or the son's revolt against his father, with the subsequent wandering in search of redemption. In the Bible, in the Book of Genesis, the story is given of Adam's sin in his rebellion against God, and of his being driven out of the Garden of Eden to wander over the unfriendly earth.

The legend of the Wanderer in Christian lore assumed distinct Christological symbols of sin and the road to redemption. The legend in this lore is invariably called "The Wandering Jew," for Jesus was a Jew and both his acceptors and rejectors were Jews. And the Wandering Jew's rejection of Jesus is the symbolical revolt against the Christian concept of redemption through Jesus, punishable by wandering in pain and in sorrow until Jesus is accepted as the Messiah.

But as the legend began to lose its mystic character and to be reinterpreted in literature, the Wanderer gradually reverted to his universal role as the symbol of the Man in search of his Soul. And the Wandering Jew —as treated by Eubule-Evans, Lysaght, and Johnson —becomes the symbol of Everyman, wandering in search of purpose and meaning to his life, until at last he realizes that what he had so long sought and yearned for is not outside but within himself. There alone he can find salvation—the Kingdom of Heaven is in his heart.

And so the legend comes to its logical end.

Bibliography

THE Legend of the Wandering Jew has been dealt with extensively in the work of theologians, chroniclers, poets, folklorists, fiction writers, and dramatists. On the general theme of guilt and redemption—which the legend symbolizes—a vast library might be assembled, with the psychoanalysts making the largest quantitative contribution.

Here are listed a few items, available in English, with comments on some that may be helpful.

There are a number of bibliographical, interpretive and fictional books on the subject in German; the subject has also been thoroughly explored in French literature; and there are a number of interesting items in Italian, Spanish, Danish and, as indicated by Yarmolinsky's bibliography, in Slavic literature. Most of these are unavailable in translation.

Baring-Gould, S. *Curious Myths of the Middle Ages*. London: Rivingstons, 1884. "The Wandering Jew" is only one of twenty-four topics treated in the book, but the book sums up the legend in its medieval form. The book also contains several myths on closely related topics, such as "The Seven Sleepers of Ephesus," "Prester John," "The Man in the Moon" (who had been exiled there for many years to be beyond the reach of death), and so on. An appendix gives a digest of the Iselandic "Braga Magus Saga" dealing with a man who grows very old, then casts off his skin and becomes young again—though this man is in no way related to Cartaphilus or Ahasuerus.

Conway, Moncure Daniel. *The Wandering Jew.* New York: Henry Holt & Company, 1881. The author of *Demonology and Devil-lore* explores the legend and its spread—broadly, if not very deeply.

Croly, George. *Salathiel: A Story of the Past, the Present and the Future.* This novel, first published in England in 1827, has since appeared in England and the United States under different titles in different editions. The Grosset & Dunlap edition of 1902 contains an introduction by Lew Wallace, author of *The Prince of India,* and twenty illustrations by T. de Thulstrup.

Doré, Gustave. *The Legend of the Wandering Jew* (see illustrations). London: Addey & Co., 1857. This particular edition is a word-for-word translation of the French edition which appeared a year earlier, and contains, in addition to the twelve Doré engravings: the poem by Pierre Dupont (trans. by George W. Thornbury); "Bibliographical Notice" by Paul Lacroix; Béranger's ballad and the music for it by Ernest Doré.

Dumas, Alexandre. *Tarry Till I Come! or The Everlasting Jew.* Trans. by F. T. Neely. Chicago, 1901.

Fleg, Edmond. *Jesus: Told by the Wandering Jew.* Trans. by Phyllis Megroz. New York: E. P. Dutton, 1935. In this novel the author skillfully reconstructs the story of the Gospels, augmented by the New Testament Apocrypha, although little is added to the legend, as such.

Franklin, Andrew. *The Wandering Jew, or Love's Masquerade,* a comedy in two acts. London, 1797.

Hoffman, David. *Chronicles of Cartaphilus, the Wandering Jew.* London: Thomas Bosworth, 1853. The full title of this work in three volumes is: *Chronicles, selected from the originals of Cartaphilus, the Wandering Jew, embracing a period of nearly XIX centuries; now first revealed to and edited by David Hoffman.* These three volumes cover only (in well over a million words) events up to the ninth century. The rest of the story was to follow in three more volumes—which were never published. Written in the form of letters, interspersed with notes and records, the book is a polychronicon, from the point of view of Cartaphilus the Wandering Jew, in which he discusses people and events throughout the centuries that in some way affected the development of Christianity, touching upon such diverse subjects as the rise and fall of empires, destiny, predestination, martyrdom of the saints, the rise of the modern Christian calendar, the doctrine of Perpetual Virginity, views of the Millennium, cabalistic philosophy, the seat of the soul, the rise of Mohammedanism, etc.

Lysaght, S.R. *The Immortal Jew,* a poetic drama in three acts. London: Macmillan and Co., Ltd., 1931. One of the most rewarding treatments of the theme of the Wanderer.

Mackinnon, David. *Ahasuerus: A Persian Play*. London, 1920.

May, Emmet Claire. *White Bears and Gold,* a collection of short stories on the Wandering Jew. Boston: R.G. Badger, 1931.

Sommerville, Maxwell. *The Wanderer's Legend*. Philadelphia: D. Biddle, 1902.

Sue, Eugène. *The Wandering Jew*. New York: Random House (Modern Library Edition G53). This long novel created a sensation when it first appeared, and continued as a best seller for many years throughout the Western world.

Thurston, E. Temple. *The Wandering Jew: A Play in Four Phases*. London, 1920. This play has often been produced in England and in the United States. In 1934 Emily Temple Thurston wrote a book based on the play, which was published by Putnam's in London.

Viereck, George Sylvester, and Eldridge, Paul. *My First Two Thousand Years: The Autobiography of the Wandering Jew*. This novel was characterized by reviewers as "an erotic interpretation of history."

The Wandering Jew: A Mythical and Aesthetical Study (no author given) with a dedication by Ambrose J. Faust. Hartford: Church Press, 1870. Primarily a theological tract.

Wallace, Lew. *The Prince of India, or Why Constantinople Fell*. New York: Harpers, 1893 (first published in 2 vols.). This novel treats the adventures of the Wandering Jew in the Byzantine Empire and is written in the style of Wallace's great success, *Ben Hur*.

Yarmolinsky, Avrahm. *The Wandering Jew*. New York, 1929. A pamphlet containing an annotated bibliography of the Legend of the Wandering Jew in Slavic literature.

Index

Other MENTOR Books of Special Interest

The Religions of Man *by Huston Smith.* The origins and basic teachings of the major faiths, from Hinduism to Christianity, by a noted scholar. (#MD253—50¢)

The Meaning of the Dead Sea Scrolls *by A. Powell Davies.* A fascinating interpretation of one of the most important archaeological discoveries of recent times. (#MD219—50¢)

The Teachings of the Mystics *by Walter T. Stace.* Selections from the writings of great mystics of both East and West, with an introductory essay on the meaning of mysticism. (#MD306—50¢)

The Dark Ages *by W. P. Ker.* A brilliant history of European literature from the fifth century to the Renaissance. (#MD225—50¢)

The Civilization of the Renaissance in Italy *by Jacob Burckhardt.* A classic that recaptures the spirit and substance of an era whose intellectual and artistic achievements have never been surpassed. Edited by Irene Gordon. (#MT321—75¢)

The Ancient Myths *by Norma Lorre Goodrich.* A vivid retelling of the great myths of Greece, Egypt, India, Persia, Crete, Sumer, and Rome. (#MD313—50¢)

A Treasury of Asian Literature *edited by John D. Yohannan.* An abundant collection of poetry, stories, and scriptures from Arabia and the Far East. (#MD243—50¢)